Successful Snooker

Successful
Snooker

Steve Davis

To my father, whose patience, coaching and support have been invaluable in helping me to master my game.

Edited by Julian Worthington

First published 1982
Reprinted 1986
by Charles Letts & Co Ltd
Diary House, Borough Road, London SE1 1DW

Consultant: John Crooke
House Editor: Liz Davies
Design: Hayward Print & Design
Illustrations: Hayward Art Group
Colour photographs: Dave Muscroft
Cover photograph: Terry Trott

ISBN 0 85097 437 2

Printed and bound by Charles Letts (Scotland) Ltd

Contents

Introduction

To get any real benefit out of this book, you must be serious about playing snooker and want to improve your game. It took years of dedication and practice to reach the standards of accuracy and consistency that helped make me a world champion. If you want to be successful at snooker, you should be aiming for this high standard. But winners aren't made overnight.

This is an instructional book, but I am not claiming that my way is the only way to play. One thing I do know, however, is that it works for me. I have tried, in the book, to show you how important the basic techniques are in building up your game; and I believe these cannot be stressed enough. Everyone will develop a certain style of his or her own. Some people are lucky and fall naturally into a good style; others have to work hard to perfect one. But the principles of technique remain the same. If you cannot grasp and execute these, you will in my opinion be making the task of improving your play that much harder.

Casual reference to the book will, of course, give you an insight into the game and how it should be played. But only with total dedication will you ever show any marked improvement or achieve any success in competitions. The main purpose of the book is to help you improve the accuracy and consistency of your cue delivery. After all, the game is basically about hitting the ball straight.

To get the right stance and cue action, you have to go right back to the beginning. You will have a better chance of starting again if you haven't got too far with your game. The longer you have been playing, the harder it will be to get rid of the bad habits and develop good ones.

I am considered to have the best cue action of all the modern day players. But if you look around you will see that no player has exactly the same style and it's not imperative for you to develop an action identical to mine. To a degree it is bound to depend on your build – whether you are tall or short, have large or small hands or a long or short reach, for example. But I believe everyone, no matter who he is,

would be a better player if he had a perfect cue action.

I spent a lot of time working on my game, analysing every aspect of it. I don't agree with those who say you can analyse all the natural ability out of yourself. Take golfers, for example. Even the best players will go back to basic techniques when things start to go wrong. I believe snooker players should adopt the same approach.

I was technically-minded from a very early stage because I wanted to make sure everything about my game was correct. And one of the secrets of being a good player is to know when things are going wrong and why. There is no point in wasting time in bad form. Because I know exactly how I play, if I go off form at all – which everyone does from time to time – I can quickly work out what is wrong and correct it. It's like knowing how your car runs. If you don't, it can take you a long time to realise something is wrong and trace the fault. Even worse, you may start to adapt to the fault and make adjustments to compensate.

Just reading the book won't make you a better player. You must practise the various points until they become second nature to you. And even when you think you have got on top of them and your game starts to improve (and with the right attitude it should), don't ignore them. From time to time it is worth forgetting about your overall game and going back to basics.

More important than anything else, practice must be fun. If you can't enjoy it, you will soon get bored with it – and inevitably your game will suffer. It always helps to have someone else interested enough to help you and tell you where you are going wrong, since a lot of faults you can't see yourself. I was fortunate that my father took such a big interest in how I played. His help was invaluable.

Enjoyment of the game is crucial, since the chances of improving are minimal once you've stopped this. How much your game improves will depend on how much you fall in love with snooker. And you will only find this out by how much you are prepared to put into it, which brings us back to groundwork. Get this right at an early stage and it will pay dividends in the long run. Certainly mastering basics is the quickest way I know of making the most of your natural ability and becoming a better player.

Work hard at the techniques and eventually you won't have to think about them. They will come naturally. Make everything a habit. Any habit is hard to get out of, so by making all your habits good ones you'll be increasing your chances of success. This is particularly true when you find yourself under pressure, since you will naturally tend to revert to your habits in that situation.

If I could spend as much time with you individually as I hope you will with my book, I would guarantee your play would improve. As it is, this book will show you how I play and what I have learnt about the game; every paragraph is an important part of the technique. Don't just read it once and leave it. Use it constantly as a reference.

Chapter 1 **Equipment**

The cue

In time the cue should become an extension of your arm, so it must suit you and feel right. For this reason you should always use your own – and look after it.

To a great extent the choice is a personal one, although there are general points worth bearing in mind. Avoid 'extremes'. Don't get a cue that is too heavy or too light, or one that is too thick or too thin. Good quality cues are made from either ash or maple; I play with an ash cue, but either is a sound choice. Ash has a strong, visible grain; with maple, the grain is less obvious. Definitely avoid cheap cues. You should always buy the best you can afford, although that doesn't mean getting one with pretty colours. These may look nice, but they don't play any better.

You can buy either one or two-piece cues; again the choice is yours. I play with a one-piece cue, the only reason being that I don't want to change a winning cue. If I had to buy one tomorrow, however, I'd definitely get a two-piece because it is far more convenient to carry around.

Make sure the cue is straight when you buy it. Most will eventually develop a slight warp, but you will find if you play regularly that you make allowances for this. Obviously there are limits to the amount a cue can bend before it becomes unusable.

Try the cue for balance. When you hold it as if to play a shot, it should feel heavy and solid in the shaft if it is perfectly balanced. Another guide is whether it balances when held at the tip end of the splice. With a badly balanced cue, the weight is more in the butt and will feel lighter when held in the playing position. If you don't have the correct weight distribution in your cue, you won't be able to play the full range of shots properly. Butt sizes tend to vary. The important thing is that the butt is not too large or small for your hand.

Make sure your cue has a ferrule fitted to the tip end. The reason for this metal or plastic ring is to help stop the end splitting and to protect it when fitting and filing a new tip.

The cue I play with is approximately 4 feet 9 inches long, weighs 17 ounces and has a 10 millimetre tip diameter. These are average measurements. Your cue does not have to be exactly the same, but I would advise you to buy one in the same range. Don't play with one whose tip is less than 10 millimetres; and unless you are 6 feet 2 inches like me, you won't need a cue quite so long. Most cues are a standard 4 feet 10 inches. If you feel the cue is too long, have it trimmed down; ideally it should reach the armpit from the floor.

Having chosen your cue, stick with it. If you get the type I have suggested and things are not going quite right with your play, then more than likely it's you and not the cue that's at fault.

Remember it is you who must decide whether the cue feels right. No one can recommend 'the right cue'. Different professionals play with different kinds; they can be 'as stiff as a poker or as flexible as a fishing rod'. You will get used to the cue the more you play with it and this is why you should always play with the same one – your own.

You'll notice that I always hold my cue with the white name plate facing up; and all top players hold their cue in a certain way for every shot. There are good reasons for this. One is that you will get used to looking at the same part of the grain for each shot. Also, if you do have a bend in the cue, you should hold it so it looks straight each time.

Looking after the cue

Look after your cue properly. Never lean it up against a wall for any length of time; it could eventually warp. Always store it flat or upright. Never leave it out in a hot place, such as in a car in warm weather; the wood will dry out and become brittle. If this happens and you drop it, it could shatter.

A cue will obviously get dirty. I wash mine down every now and again with warm water and then rub it dry. Very occasionally I also rub in a little linseed oil to stop the wood going brittle.

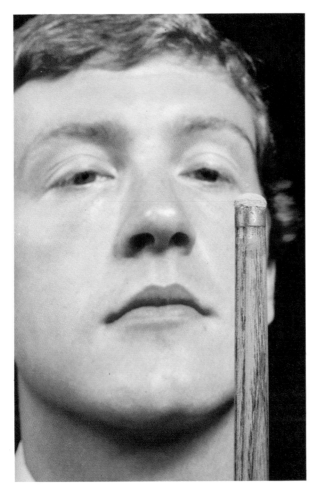

Fig. 1 *The cue tip. Notice how it has been dome-shaped, although this should not be too exaggerated.*

The tip

You need a certain amount of resilience at the striking end of the cue in order to grip the ball, and this is why you have a leather tip. There are many makes; I use either Elk Master or Blue Diamond.

Always play with a firm tip – not too soft or rock hard – although you can never really tell what a tip will be like until you've played with it. The tip must always have some give in it. A rock hard one, which is too compressed, will not grip the ball – and will have a similar effect as playing with no tip at all. If the tip is too soft, it will compress so much when you hit the ball that you'll have less 'feel' and certain shots – especially those with side – will be virtually unplayable.

Remember it is more important to have a perfect tip on a reasonable cue than a bad tip on a perfect cue. After all, it's the tip that hits the ball.

The life of a tip obviously depends on how much you play. Some players like to file their tips right down or play with old ones. This obviously means a shorter life, but the tip is then usually at its best for playing – as long as it doesn't get too hard. Only with practice will you find out what tip suits you best.

If you get into the habit of holding the cue the same way, you will get uneven wear on the tip – especially the part that is used for screw shots – and it will look lopsided. But you shouldn't worry about this because the tip will wear naturally.

Retipping the cue

Learn how to put on your own tips. If you do it yourself, you will take pride in the job and ensure it is done properly. File the bottom surface of the tip and the end of the cue to make sure they are flat and clean. I use a quick-drying adhesive which allows me to test the tip straight away and change it if necessary.

Having stuck on the tip, you will have to trim it down to size and dome the top (Fig. 2). Always file down on the tip to prevent ripping it off the cue. If it becomes shiny with use and won't hold chalk, you can rough up the surface slightly by tapping a file on it.

This will help it hold chalk. Don't use sandpaper as this tends to tear the leather.

The chalk

I – and most top players – use green Triangle chalk. You can get blue, but green is preferable because it doesn't show up so much on the cue ball or the table.

Whichever type you use, make sure it is not cakey or powdery; you ought to be able to hear the chalk going on. When you apply it, wipe it once or twice across the surface of the tip; never grind it in.

Chalk helps improve the grip on the ball; without it you would be restricted to playing centre-ball shots. As I have already said, the shinier the leather, the less grip you get. If the chalk is too powdery, it won't hold to the tip so well and again will impair the grip on the ball.

Make a habit of applying chalk after each shot, particularly when playing side, screw or other advanced shots. It is not quite so vital for a plain-ball shot, but get into the habit of chalking regularly nevertheless.

The table

Tables are covered in green cloth, have cushions on each side and six pockets and the standard size is 12 feet × 6 feet. But that is where the similarity between tables ends, since every table has its own characteristics and plays slightly differently. There are few tables that do not, after several years' wear and tear, develop idiosyncracies; the most common of all is not being level.

There are many factors affecting the way a table will play. These include temperature, humidity, whether the cloth is new or worn and the wear on the cushions. A worn cloth will lose its nap, so it is best to practise on a table with as new a cloth as possible. The effects of the nap – and the cushions – will be explained later.

Try to play on as many different tables as possible, so you get used to playing under different conditions.

Fig. 2 *When shaping the tip, always file downwards to prevent lifting the tip off the end of the cue.*

11

Ideally you should start on a fairly lively table with at least standard size pockets. The bigger the pockets, the more confidently you will pot balls and therefore the quicker you can concentrate on positional play.

Pocket sizes vary from table to table, although they are becoming more uniform. For matchplay the pockets have to be a standard size and they are measured with a template.

Avoid playing too much on a table with small pockets. This will tend to cramp your game and encourage you to put too much emphasis on potting and less on positional play. And it is the latter that's so vital for break-building once you have passed the elementary stage.

Very few tables are absolutely level and the danger of playing on the same table all the time is that you will adjust your shots accordingly and you will have problems readjusting on a different table.

If you always play on a slow table, you will get accustomed to hitting the ball hard and once again you will have problems readjusting to a faster table. Equally, if you play too much on a fast table, you will tend to tap at the ball instead of striking it. Try to play on all types and see what the differences are.

I started playing on a quarter-size table. This is ideal practice ground for youngsters who cannot, for any reason, get on larger size tables. The quality of these is getting better all the time and they are certainly adequate for practising the basic techniques.

Looking after the table

Although the table you play on is probably not your own, you should always treat it as such and remember that other players will be following you and will want to enjoy it as well. It is obvious, but I must say it, that you should never drink or smoke over the table. As far as other damage is concerned, beginners are often frightened of tearing the cloth; in fact, there is little chance of this happening with normal treatment. Avoid sitting on the cushions, since these are only bolted on to the side of the table.

Ideally the table should be brushed from baulk end to black spot end every day and ironed twice a week to keep the nap down; this makes the table play faster. Brushing is important to bring up the nap and to prevent dust collecting in the cloth.

Before striking the ball

Everything you start to do that changes your technique will seem uncomfortable at first, but as you get used to it the new method will become second nature. So persevere and don't be tempted to slip back into what feels comfortable but is probably the wrong way of doing it.

The grip

I use the word 'grip' reluctantly because it could give you the wrong idea of how to hold the cue correctly.

I hold the cue with my thumb and first two fingers. The other two fingers are just resting against the cue at this stage. There should be no tension in the hand; the cue should be held loosely but securely. Make sure

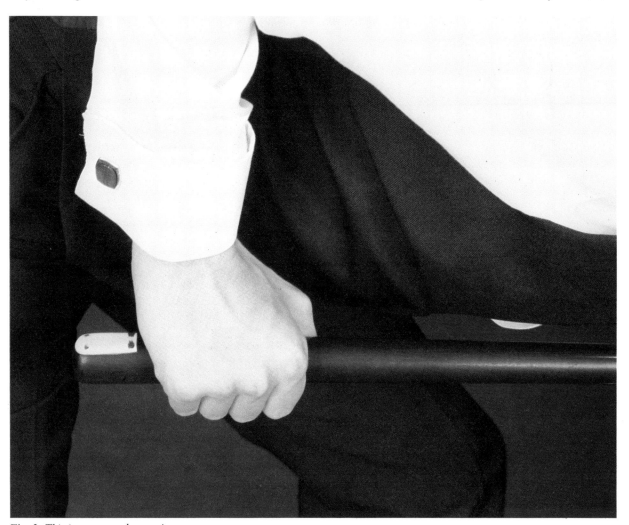

Fig. 3 *This is my normal cue grip.*

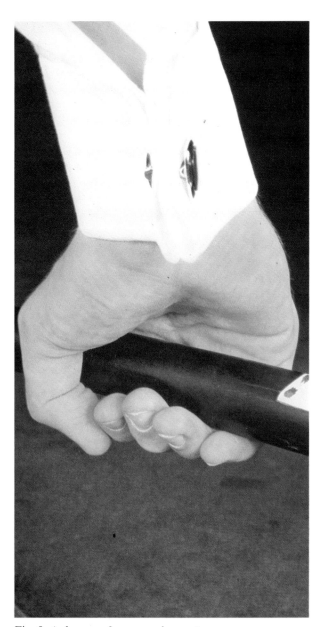

Fig. 4 *The end view of my normal cue grip. Notice how the wrist is locked with the arm to prevent any side wobble.*

Fig. 5 *A close-up of my normal cue grip.*

the grip is only firm enough to stop the cue sliding about in the hand.

You will find as you strike the cue ball that your fingers tighten up and the hold becomes more of a 'grip' – better explained as a slight squeeze. If you grip the cue too tightly to start with, you will not be able to tighten it later and will lose a lot of the necessary feeling of the shot that comes with this 'squeeze'.

Although it is not considered textbook practice, I tend to cock my wrist outwards slightly. I have tried playing with my wrist vertical, but for me there seemed to be too much wobble. To compensate I had to grip the cue tighter, which obviously I didn't want to do. My wrist is locked as a single unit with my arm, although my grip on the cue is still relaxed. I would not necessarily advise you to copy me, however. If you can hang your wrist vertically without gripping the cue tightly and feel you still have control of the cue, then do so.

In the rest position, the line of the knuckles should be roughly horizontal to the ground in line with the cue. The position of these will alter fractionally as you play the shot and I will explain this later when I come to the action of the right arm. The grip alters very slightly as the cue is moved backwards and forwards prior to the shot. This is to compensate for the change in angle the cue makes with the forearm.

Obviously the size of your hand could affect the grip and it is therefore important to have the right size butt to hold comfortably.

Where you grip the cue will depend to an extent on the type of shot you are playing and where you have your bridge in relation to the cue ball. It will also depend on the length of the cue. This highlights the importance of having a cue that is the right length for you; otherwise you will be restricted when playing certain shots.

Normally my grip is about 3 inches from the end of the cue. There are times, however, when I hold the cue right at the end and tuck my little finger around the back of the butt. This is a very comfortable grip and

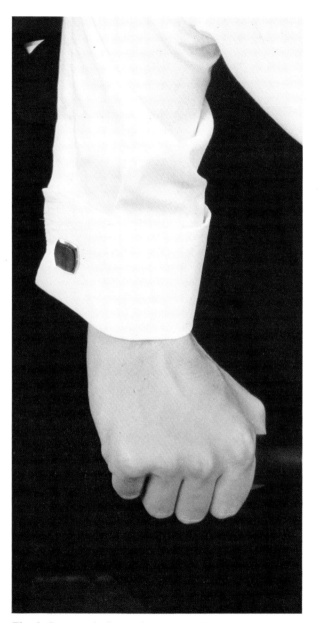

Fig. 6 *Gripping the butt end of the cue. There is no basic difference in this grip, but some people do find it more comfortable.*

can be used if you are playing a power shot or need a longer distance between the bridge and the cue ball. Never hold the butt end if you have more cue beyond the bridge than normal, since this tends to affect your accuracy when striking, as you will see later.

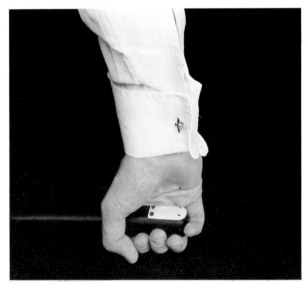

Fig. 7 *A close-up of the butt-end grip. My wrist does not hang vertically when I grip the cue, but I find with this grip I feel more in control of the cue.*

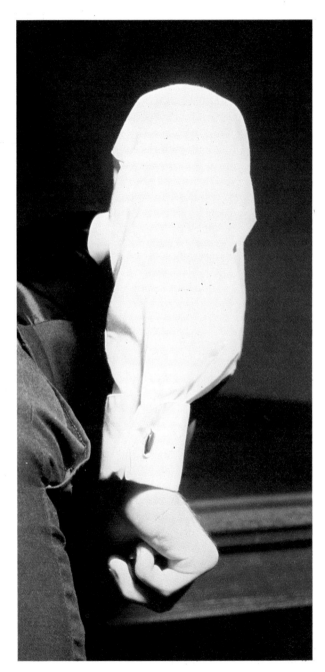

Fig. 8 *Notice how the little finger wraps round the butt when gripping the end of the cue.*

The feet

The feet are a vital part of the overall stance when you get down to play a shot. You must have a solid base on which to build. Although you don't have to stand in exactly the same way as I do, you should adopt the principles on stance which I am going to describe.

When you approach the table, the right foot should be on line with the shot, with the toes pointing slightly outwards. Your left foot should be at least 12 inches from the right one to give you a solid stance. The toes should be pointing roughly in line with the shot. The back of the foot should be on a line with the back of the right foot that creates an angle of about 60 degrees with the direction of the shot. This is, of course, an approximate guide and inevitably will depend on what is a comfortable position. But never stray too far from it.

Familiarise yourself with this position. You will not be able to check it every time you play, but after a while you should find yourself doing it naturally without even thinking about it. I find this position not only gives me a firm base, but also the best balance for the shot. I lock the right leg straight to make sure it is anchored firmly to the ground. The left leg is bent and balances the rest of the body, which is to the left of the shot.

You may well want to change this angle slightly and, in fact, many experts suggest standing at 45 degrees to the shot and twisting into the shot to create certain tensions in the body. I find the squarer you stand to the shot, the greater your resistance to sideways movement, which would otherwise cause you to miss the shot. By the same token, you cannot stand with the feet level since the left side of the body must be well in front of the right.

When playing a shot, you will have three points of contact with the ground. The two legs, as described, take most of the weight. The third point of contact is the bridge (via the table, of course), which takes a small amount of weight. If you take your bridge away suddenly, you should just be starting to fall forwards

Fig. 9 *One way of making sure you are adopting the correct stance is to mark the floor where you are taking up position for the shot; you can do this using either three cues or some strips of white tape. Place one cue in line with the line of the shot and put your right foot in position behind this cue. Place another cue at right angles to the line of the shot at the back of your right foot. Lay the third cue so it crosses the second cue at the back of the right foot at an angle of approximately 30 degrees to the second cue. Then position your left foot so the back of it touches this third cue at least 12 inches from the right foot.*

17

on to the table. You should not be leaning so far forward that you are uncomfortable. Don't lean back on your right leg, since your balance would be in the opposite direction to the shot. As a guide, you won't be far wrong if your right leg is vertical to the ground.

The bridge

The bridge is one of only two contacts you have with the cue and must be as solid as the name suggests.

Place the left hand, which will form the bridge, on the table and spread out the fingers as wide as they will

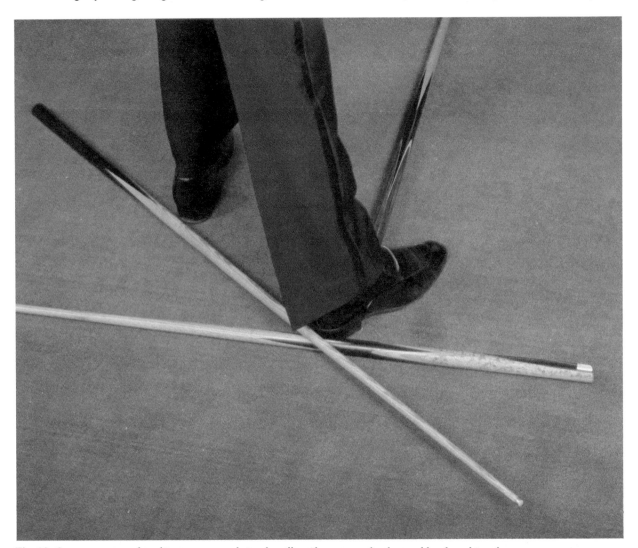

Fig. 10 *Once you get used to this stance, you obviously will not have to go the the trouble of marking the floor, which incidentally will be a lot easier if you have someone to help you.*

go. Compress the finger pads against the cloth – and as much of the finger below the pads as you can. The narrower the span of your bridge, the wobblier and rockier it will be and you certainly don't want any sideways movement as you play the shot. Make sure the base of your hand grips the cloth firmly as well. This may not always be possible, but I will say more about awkward bridges later.

Bring your thumb in as tight as you can to the forefinger and cock it up as much as possible. I am fortunate in that my thumb is double-jointed, so I can cock it up high and make a really deep 'V' shape groove through which the cue will slide.

Start to grip the cloth with the finger pads and you will automatically lift up the knuckles. But keep the base of the hand down on the table. The more contact with the cloth you have, the better your bridge will be.

A point worth mentioning here is that you can ease the pressure on the outside of the hand or lift it slightly, for example, when you want to play a screw shot, but the inside of the hand must always remain firm on the table. The bridge acts as a guideline for the cue. Within reason, the nearer it is to the cue ball, the more accurate the shot should be, since you will be reducing the margin for error between the bridge and the white. To illustrate this point, move your bridge up the cue and then move the butt end about. The tip of the cue will move further in relation to the amount the butt end moves.

Equally, the closer the bridge is to the white, the more cramped you will be to the shot and the less back swing you can play with. The back swing is important when you come to play smooth, controlled shots and power shots. Basically make your bridge the minimum distance from the cue ball that feels comfortable for the shot you want to play. In normal circumstances my bridge is no closer than 9 inches and usually about 12 inches from the white.

Another important reason for having the bridge a reasonable distance from the cue ball is that it seems easier to sight the ball. Another aid to sighting is the

Fig. 11 *From this head-on view of my normal bridge, you will notice how the fingers are spread, with as much of the finger pads gripping the cloth as possible. Make sure you have a strong 'V' for the cue when you cock your thumb.*

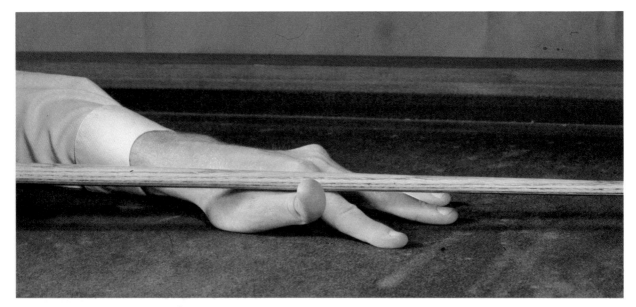

Fig. 12 *My normal bridge seen side-on.*

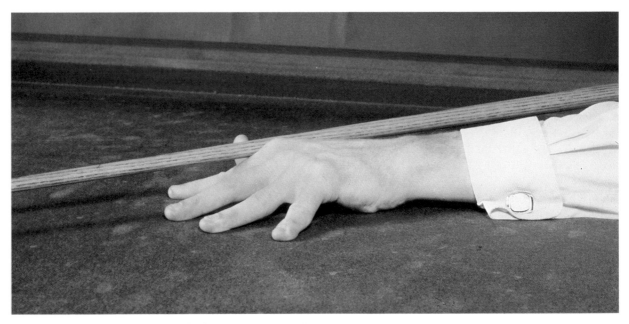

Fig. 13 *Notice here how the pads of the fingers and the base of the hand grip the cloth.*

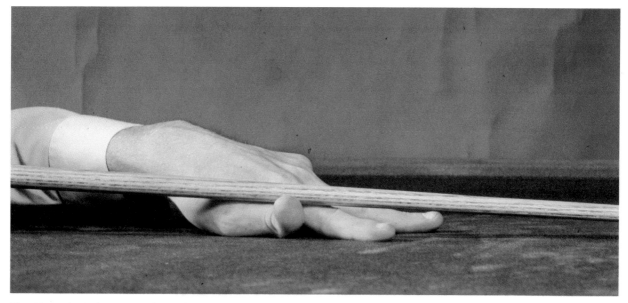

Fig. 14 *Bridging for a screw shot. The whole hand is lowered, with the thumb almost on the cloth.*

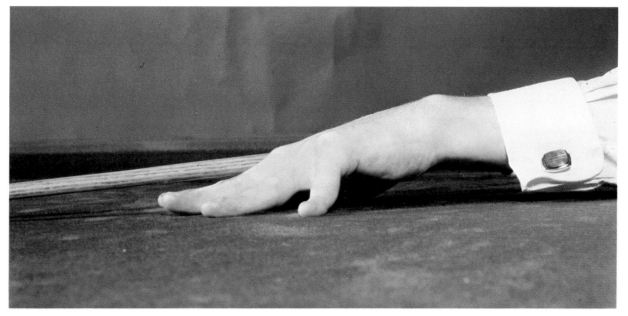

Fig. 15 *A side-on view of the bridge for a screw shot. The hand is twisted over to lower the bridge.*

backward and forward movement of the cue while cueing up, since you can check if your cue is running straight. With too short a bridge you can't draw the cue back far enough to check for any error.

As I have already mentioned, your bridge will be longer when you play a power shot because you will need a greater back swing. But this will tend to reduce your accuracy, so take a lot of care when playing this type of shot.

I said that the position of the bridge depends on the position of the cue ball on the table. If this is less than 12 inches from a cushion and the shot you want to play is roughly square to the table, you will have to shorten your bridge. The closer the ball is to a cushion, the more difficult and restricted your cueing will be.

You will see from Figs. 16 to 20 how I have had to alter my bridge the closer the cue ball gets to the cushion. Playing it from the yellow position, I can use a normal bridge. From the green position, I have had

to raise the base of the hand from the table, but otherwise the bridge is still a normal one. From the brown position, I have taken my thumb out of the way and used it as additional support on the side of the table. The forefinger is looped over the cue and acts as a guide, together with the middle finger. In the blue position the cue is resting on the table and my thumb and forefinger form a channel for the cue. In the pink position the area I can hit on the cue ball is limited and, therefore, I have to raise the butt of my cue slightly to avoid miscueing. This time the cue runs in the 'V' of the thumb and forefinger and not on the cushion.

The closer to the cushion you get, the more you will have to raise the bridge, the less of the cue ball you will see and the higher up you must hit it. If you want to play a power shot with the ball in this position, you will have to move the hand right back to the edge of the table with only the finger pads supporting the bridge. This is a particularly tricky bridge since you

Fig. 16 *The colours are positioned to indicate where you have to alter the normal bridge when playing the cue ball near the cushion. Bridge normally from the yellow; from the green the base of the hand is raised.*

Fig. 17 *From the brown, the forefinger is hooked over the cue and the thumb grips the side of the table.*

have so little of the hand gripping the table and you must keep the whole hand rigid. In the black position, as with the pink, you will have a limited back swing, which in turn will restrict the range of shots you can play – as well as making whatever shot you play that much harder. I have got all the pressure on the finger pads at the back edge of the table.

There is an alternative form of bridge for some awkward shots which a few players use. It's the loop bridge, where the forefinger forms a loop over the cue,

23

Fig. 18 *From the blue the cue rests on the table and the thumb and forefinger act as a guide.*

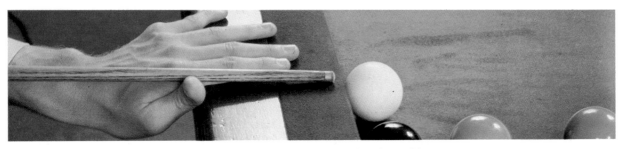

Fig. 19 *From the black (as with the pink), your hand rests on the back edge of the table.*

Fig. 20 *If you want to play a power shot in this position only the finger pads will support the bridge.*

which rests on the thumb. I personally limit the use of this bridge to when I am playing a shot down the cushion. The loop bridge does mean you can lower the cue more, which helps for screw shots and in some people's opinion guarantees less cue wobble. But I find it tends to obstruct my line of vision down the cue. I would suggest, therefore, that you limit its use, unless of course you find you can play with it more successfully.

Probably the most demanding bridge is the one when you are trying to hit the cue ball with another ball in the way of the shot. However the same principles apply. Keep as much of the ends of the fingers on the cloth as you can, with the fingers well spread and

25

Fig. 21 *One of the many variations of bridge when you cannot use the normal bridge to play a shot. The important point about bridging is to be able to adapt the bridge wherever you are on the table.*

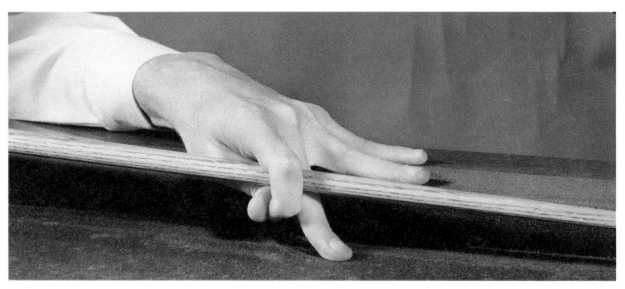

Fig. 22 *Another variation is the looped bridge, which can be used when you cannot get your hand on the table for a normal bridge – for example, along the cushion.*

26

Fig. 23 *Bridging over a ball. This is one of the trickiest bridges, since your hand must clear the intervening ball, which means it is up in the air. Notice here how firmly the pads of the fingers are gripping the cloth; these are your only means of support. Otherwise, the bridge is similar to a normal one in that your fingers must be well spread out and the thumb and forefinger form a deep 'V' for the cue. The great danger here is of miscueing, since you will be hitting down on the ball and having to aim near the top of the ball. Take time with the bridge and, above all, make sure you feel comfortable. Although the position is slightly awkward, with practice you should get used to it and not be afraid to play this type of shot.*

the thumb tight to the forefinger and cocked to form a good grove. Your hand will, of course, be up in the air.

The key to this type of bridge is to have it as firm and as comfortable as possible. You will be tending to hit down on the ball, aiming nearer the top of it (as you do when hitting a ball tight to the cushion). Therefore great care is needed since a miscue is more likely here.

Fig. 24 *When bridging over a ball, make sure the arm is kept in line with the cue and the line of the shot.*

27

Fig. 25 *When bridging over a ball, make sure you gain the necessary height. You may even have to lift the back leg off the floor. This of course weakens the stance, so greater care is needed to avoid errors.*

Fig. 26 *Occasionally, when you need to bridge over a ball in the middle of the table and have to get as much height as possible, you can play the shot sitting on the edge of the table. Remember, however, that one foot must still be touching the floor.*

Hints on practice

Get the feel of playing the cue ball off the cushion.

Put it tight against the bottom cushion behind the brown spot and practise hitting it straight into the two top pockets in turn. When you can do this consistently, try the harder shot of potting the cue ball into each of the two middle pockets in turn.

Fig. 27 *There are times when, to play an awkward shot, you have to take one leg off the floor. Here the left leg is on the edge of the table; this helps keep the stance as solid as possible.*

Fig. 28 *When playing a shot with one leg on the table, make sure you still feel comfortable and check that you have not impeded your cueing action.*

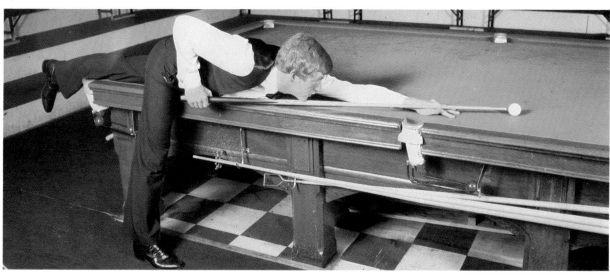

Left arm

The position of your left arm is important and does, to an extent, affect your bridge. I have mine bent at the elbow, with as much of the forearm on the table as possible. This gives me added support and provides a more solid base for the bridge.

The traditional theory is that your left arm should be thrust out straight and rigid. However I find, as I am tall, that this tends to cramp my action and cause all sorts of problems. With the left arm bent, I find my technique is much more compact and comfortable and I have more of my left arm acting as a brace on the table.

The middle fingers of your bridge should be pointing roughly in line with the shot. With the arm bent at the elbow, you have to twist the left hand slightly to bring it into line with the cue. The other great advantage about bending my left arm is that it enables my cue to run freely, unobstructed by my body, and allows my right arm to be perfectly in line with the cue.

Right arm

This is the part of the body that does the real business – controlling and directing the cue. It seems to me the easiest way to cue straight is to have all the arm in line with the cue – and the shot. Then it is just a matter of pivoting it at the elbow. When in the rest position, you should have the right forearm vertical to the floor. I will discuss this further when I talk about the cue action.

If you don't have your right arm lined up with the cue, it seems to me you are complicating the action of moving the cue in a straight line. At this stage I must stress that the simpler the technique, in whatever you are doing, the less chance there is of making errors. Part of the essence of successful snooker, as with any other game, is keeping the chance of mistakes to a minimum.

What happens if I don't have my right arm directly in line with the cue and the line of the shot? If my

Fig. 29 *A head-on view of the cueing-up position. Notice that the line from the right shoulder through to the arm is straight and in line with the cue and the left forearm is completely on the table to give the bridge support.*

Fig. 30 *The cueing-up position seen from the back. Again you can see how a straight line is formed from the right elbow through to the tip of the cue.*

elbow is tucked in, my cue tends to arc as it moves forward and ends up hitting the ball on the left. If my elbow is sticking out, my cue goes to the right. Of course, if I played long enough like this I would learn to compensate for it. I find it is worth my while to keep my arm absolutely in line. Some players have the cue parallel but directly in line. This too adds complications for which compensation has to be made. If I am under pressure in a match and am not hitting the ball so 'sweetly', I have a better chance of still making the shot than a player with an inferior alignment.

Let's go back to why your right forearm should hang vertically, since if it doesn't this can impose restrictions on your range of shots.

If you grip the cue with your arm forward of vertical when in the rest position, you will be able to swing back further. But you will be restricting your follow-through and you will tend to lift the cue off the bridge as you play the shot. To counteract this, you would have to drop your elbow to get the required follow-through. As in all ball games, follow-through plays a vital part, which I will discuss later.

If you grip the cue backward of vertical, you will tend to lift the butt end as you pull it back. On your follow-through, when the arm reaches the vertical position, the tip of the cue would be higher than intended. To compensate for this, you will have to raise your elbow in conjunction with the follow-through, once again introducing another variable into the cue action.

One small point. Some experts believe the cue should rub against the chest. The theory behind this is that the chest acts as another guide point for the cue and tends to steady it up. When I tried this, I found myself hitting my rib cage with my knuckles. This bruised me so much after a week that I started to arc the cue round the chest in a right-to-left movement to prevent any more pain. You may find it is an advantage to have another guideline for the cue, but you may agree I have proved it's not necessary.

When playing a shot, the right arm has three

31

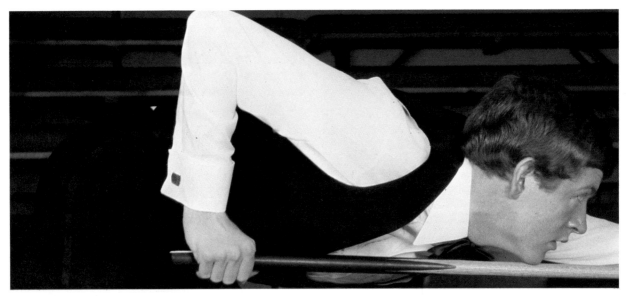

Fig. 31 *The rest position, the first of the three stages in the cueing action.*

Fig. 32 *The back-swing position – the second stage. You can see how the line of the knuckles alters only slightly and, most important, the elbow through to the shoulder remains in the same position.*

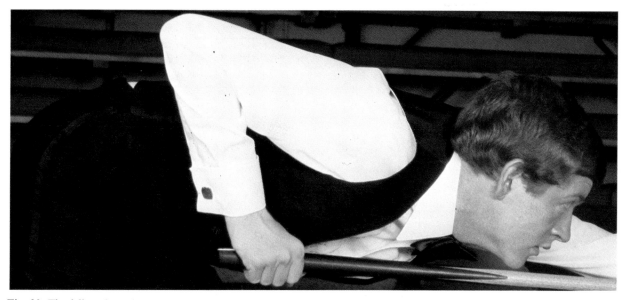

Fig. 33 *The follow-through position – the final stage. The elbow drops only fractionally.*

Fig. 34 *The three positions of the cueing action together. From this you can clearly see how little movement there is in the upper part of the arm.*

definite positions which I shall call the rest, back swing and follow-through. I will be dealing with these in detail when I talk about cueing up.

As I have said, you should have your right forearm vertical to the ground in the rest position and the knuckles of the hand parallel to the ground. From this point you should move the right arm like a piston, pivoting it at the elbow but keeping the elbow, as much as possible, in the same position. When you reach the full extent of the back swing, the knuckles will be pointing down slightly. As you move the cue forward to the full extent of the follow-through, the line of the knuckles will point up a fraction and the back of the palm will come down on to the cue.

Fig. 35 The complete stance. Notice that the back leg is straight and slightly forward into the shot, the right forearm is perpendicular to the floor and the cue is kept as low and horizontal as possible.

Striking the ball

The next stage of the game, once you have mastered all aspects of the stance and getting down to the shot, is striking the ball successfully. This means hitting the cue ball in the desired direction. It may surprise you to know that there is probably as much involved in this as in the rest of the basic techniques put together. Certainly it is true if you want to be able to do this accurately and consistently.

Most reasonable players can do this satisfactorily. But the big difference between them and the top players is greater consistency, allied with the fact that the better players are those who can cue accurately under pressure. If you develop a really sound cue action, this will tend to sustain you even if your nerve starts to weaken. And there is no better way of exploiting any natural ability than by first developing a good action.

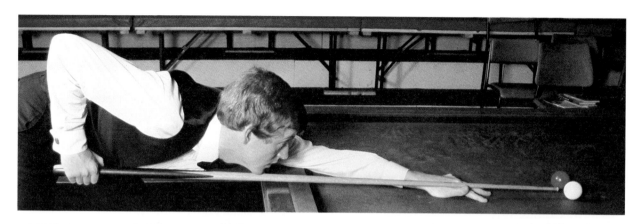

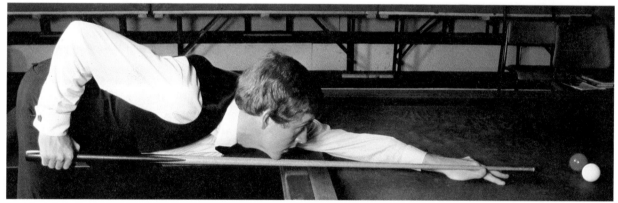

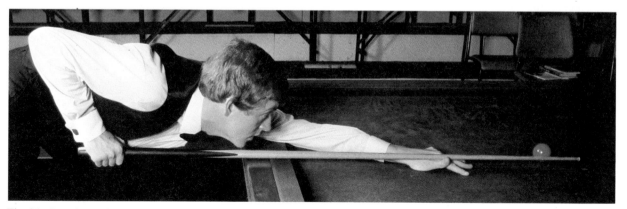

Fig. 36 *Complete side-on views of the three positions through the cueing action – rest, back-swing and follow-through. Throughout the action, make sure you keep your head still and in the same position.*

Hints on practice

Practise hitting the cue ball up and down the spots.

Put it on the brown spot and strike it straight up the table, over the blue, pink and black spots on to the top cushion and back over the spots.

Vary the speed at which you strike the cue ball and check how accurately you strike it. The harder you hit it, the more deviation you are likely to get.

There are no other balls in the way to look at, so keep your eye on the blue spot as you pause before the strike. If the cue ball doesn't come back over the spots, check you are cueing straight and that you are striking the cue ball in the middle.

If you can do this successfully 10 times in succession, you should be well on the way to successful potting.

At this stage put the blue on its spot and line up the white for a full-ball pot into each of the top corner pockets in turn. The line of the shot should be the diagonal of the table from the bottom right-hand pocket to the top left-hand pocket – and vice-versa – with the white and object ball in that line. Try to pot the blue. If you can do this 10 times out of 10 you are a better player than me!

This exercise may sound ridiculously simple, but it can be very helpful for a beginner who lacks confidence and is not yet playing smoothly, usually because he is frightened of having to pot balls as well as strike the white correctly.

Put the white on the brown spot and try potting it into all the pockets in turn. Concentrate on the basic techniques of cue action and striking the ball that I have discussed.

Cue action

The closer your action is to the 'piston and rifle' principle (which, incidentally, Joe Davis used as an example in his book), the better your game will be. I'll explain.

The piston works on the principle of consistent backward and forward motion in a predetermined line. If you imagine the arm as a piston rod and the cue as the piston, you should begin to see what I mean. In the same way, imagine the bridge – or more correctly the 'V' of the bridge – as the sight on a rifle. In effect you are pushing the cue through the bridge along the sight line towards the target, in this case the object ball. Just as the piston operates in a regular to and fro motion, so should the cue. With a rifle you should not move your body at all when firing, and so with the cue you should keep completely still on the shot.

As with sighting up a rifle, so with a cue keep your eyes as low as possible to the line of the cue and behind the white. For normal shots, hold the cue as horizontal as possible, with your head low down over it. One of the most frequent causes of a mis-shot is lifting up your head, with the result that the body is allowed to move. By concentrating on keeping your head still and low during and after the shot, you will almost be able to guarantee absolute stillness throughout cue delivery.

To get your eyes as close to the line of the cue as possible, the cue should brush your chin. After a period of time, I even got a scar on mine. I'm not suggesting that you have to suffer these agonies to become a useful player. But it was a good, if painful, reminder that I was keeping my head down. With perfect eyesight your head will be central over the cue. Obviously the state of people's eyes varies a lot and you will naturally sight with the strongest eye.

The crucial point I am making here is to keep the head anchored down over the cue throughout the whole shot. My father used to stand over me with his cue held a fraction above my head when I played a shot. If I lifted it, I touched the cue – and failed the test.

Once again I must stress the importance of keeping the head down even after the shot has been played. This will ensure that you follow through correctly. Lots of players tend to lift their head as they strike the ball – and with it the cue as well. Wait until the ball has gone into the pocket – or at the very least until the white has struck the object ball – before allowing yourself to lift it. Exaggerate this until it becomes second nature.

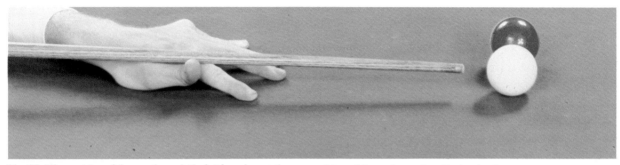

Fig. 37 *The position of the cue through the bridge when at the rest position of the cueing action. Notice the tip of the cue is not too close to the cue ball at this stage.*

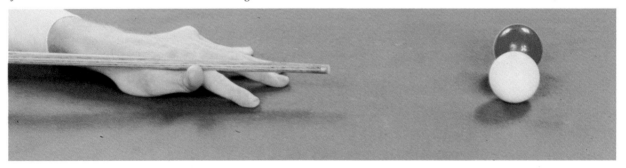

Fig. 38 *The position of the cue through the bridge when at the back-swing position.*

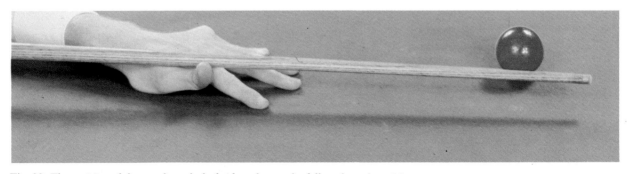

Fig. 39 *The position of the cue through the bridge when at the follow-through position*

37

Hints on practice

Use a mirror to get a reflection of your action, so you can look at it and see where you are going wrong.

Stand a large mirror on a chair against the side of the table. Place the white in the middle of the table and aim to hit its reflection in the mirror full-ball.

Not only will you be able to see if your arm is in line with the cue, but you can also see whether the two cues are lined up before you hit the white – and afterwards, as well. By this you can tell whether the cue is going through absolutely straight or with an arcing action.

Cueing up on the white

Apart from making sure you have a comfortable bridge, the only things you should be concentrating on are the white and the object ball.

A good tip is to stand in line with the shot for a moment before you get down. Don't – as you sometimes see players doing – walk round the table and get straight down to play the shot. You should have worked out the angle at which you want to strike the object ball, where you want to send it (into the pocket, hopefully) and what type of shot you want to play *before* you get down.

First and foremost, you must prepare yourself mentally for the shot. Steady yourself up, make sure you are in a comfortable position and give your eyes time to look at both the white and the object ball.

When you are satisfied you are in the correct position, start to move the cue backwards and forwards over the bridge. This should be a smooth movement, since the object is to work up the right rhythm, without which you can never hope to have proper control over the white. You can always tell a good player by how smoothly and confidently he goes through this preliminary motion. And don't think this is just for show, because it's not. It's all part of playing the shot in exactly the right way, just as darts or golf players do before letting go of a dart or striking a golf ball. It's a very deliberate and planned action.

On the other hand, don't overdo it or prolong it more than is necessary. Remember, you are in a position that will eventually become a strain after too long and you may well pass your peak before you have made your shot. I knew a player who moved his cue backwards and forwards no fewer than 24 times before he finally hit the ball. In fact he was a good player, but I certainly wouldn't recommend that you copied his example.

All the time you are going through this movement, you should be checking that your cue is travelling through in a straight line to where you want to hit the cue ball.

When you are ready to strike the ball, it is extremely important that you pause on the final back swing. I find it virtually impossible to complete the final back swing and thrust forward in the same movement and keep it rhythmic. This pause lasts just a split second, but you will find it makes a difference. It also allows you a fraction more time to fix your eyes on the object ball. But don't pause so long that you hesitate over striking the ball.

The preparation and timing involved is all-important if you want to strike the ball accurately and effectively. Whatever you do, never walk up to the table, get down and go 'one, two, bang.' If you can't break that habit, you might as well stop reading now.

Eyes

While all this is going on, what should the eyes be doing? And which ball should the eyes finally be on when you strike the white? The answer to the second question is, 'on the object ball'. This is, in fact, where a lot of people go wrong. Some concentrate on the cue ball to check they are striking it in the right place, while others are already looking at the pocket to see where the object ball is going. You mustn't do either.

Having selected the line of the shot from behind the white and the angle at which you want to strike the object ball, get down and cue up for the shot. At this stage you should look at the white to make sure where on that ball your cue will strike. Then look along the line of the cue, from behind the bridge past the tip to the white and follow on with your eyes to the part of the object ball you want to hit. It is not an easy thing to do, but try to visualise the white actually hitting the object ball. Of course, all this should be happening as you go through the backward and forward movement with your cue.

Flick your eyes backwards and forwards to double-check where you will be striking both the white and the object ball. By now the pocket is irrelevant and you should not throw your eyes off line to look at it.

When you start the final back swing, your eyes should be on the white, but beginning to move on to the object ball, so that by the time you pause for the final thrust forward your eyes are firmly fixed on the latter. More precisely, you should be concentrating on that part of the object ball you want to hit with the white.

If at any stage during this you don't feel quite right or comfortable, get up from the table and start again. Never try making conscious adjustments (for example, moving your cue about) at this late stage. Imperceptibly you will probably be making very slight adjustments all the time.

It is important to fix your eyes on the object ball when you strike the white because you will automatically send the cue in the direction you are looking. Never be caught with your eyes looking halfway between the white and the object ball. The arm will naturally follow the line of the shot to the object ball if that is where you are looking. It's rather like a radar tracking device.

If you can synchronise the pause and where your eyes should be looking, you will have achieved something that took me hours of frustration and practice.

And that's not the end of it. After you have struck the cue ball, try to keep your eyes fixed on the spot where the object ball was, even after it has moved off. There is a natural tendency to let your eyes follow the object ball once it has been struck. Eventually you could start to lift your eyes before hitting the white, which could be fatal.

I cannot stress enough the importance of having your eyes fixed on the right ball at the right time. In a normal ball game, you would naturally look at the ball you are hitting or kicking. But snooker's totally different, basically because there are two balls involved. If I'm mistiming the ball, it's usually because I've made my final movement forward before my eyes were fixed on the object ball. That's how important it is to watch the right ball.

It will take you a long time to get into the habit of using this sequence when cueing up. When you've got to grips with it, however, you will do it without even thinking about it – and I believe it is the whole secret of timing the ball perfectly. Only when you have mastered this will you have a guarantee of getting some consistency into your game.

Cue delivery

When you strike the cue ball, it must be a deliberate, confident and positive action. Don't be frightened of striking the ball. If you are, you will almost certainly not deliver the cue properly.

The way you actually hit the cue ball is, in effect, more like a punch. The theory is similar to that of striking a golf ball. The cue should be moving at its fastest just after it has struck the ball. This way you will achieve the maximum amount of power with the least effort. The more effort you have to put into any shot, the greater the chance of movement or error.

Some days you will find your timing is out – and this will be mainly due to the way you are striking the ball. Sometimes it seems to take so much effort, while at other times it is almost effortless.

If your basic technique is right, you should be

able to analyse quite easily why you are not striking correctly. Usually it is because you are not pausing effectively after the final back swing or your eyes are not on the right ball at the right time. The pause becomes vital for consistent timing. The final movement through after the pause is a definite thrust – not a push, lunge or jerk.

If you can get into the habit of striking the ball as confidently as if all you had to do was hit it straight into a pocket, you will have achieved the right striking action. The doubts usually come when you start to worry about where the object ball is going.

Another fault that will impair the effectiveness of the final thrust is if you over-lengthen the back swing. This will tend to slow down the final forward movement of the cue. Without feeling you are jerking at the shot, keep the back swing to the minimum required to create the power you need for the shot. In a way, it's like a bowler in cricket. The extent of the run-up will be dictated by the intended speed of the delivery.

Most technical books on the game emphasize the follow-through – and I agree that it plays a very important part in striking the ball accurately. This is particularly true for advanced shots when any type of spin is required. But don't go through the motions just for the sake of it. At first, I tried to follow through because I read how important it was, but without really understanding why. This resulted in my pushing the ball rather than striking it. When I then saw the top players punching the ball and following through automatically, I realised that this was a natural thing that happened as part of a complete movement.

I cannot emphasise enough this final back swing, pause and strike. Most players have certain idiosyncracies in their initial cueing-up; but the good players are sorted out from the bad by the way they play this final sequence. If you concentrate on the way you strike the ball, positively rather than with a half-hearted push, you will find the follow-through becomes a natural part of your action. Compare a punch in boxing, for example. You don't aim to punch as far as the contact with the body and then stop – anticipating resistance. You must punch through and beyond the point of contact.

A final reminder once you have struck the ball. As I said earlier, you must keep the cue at its finishing point since this ensures a good follow-through. Also make sure you keep your head still since it is much more difficult to go through with the shot correctly if you move it. If you do not keep your head still you will need more compensation in your action to keep the cue on the correct horizontal path.

Although I will be discussing side and how to play it later, here is one example of how follow-through can affect a shot. If, when hitting with side, you just jab at the cue ball and don't follow through, you will get side. But it won't be nearly as much as you may want nor will you push the white as far off course as you would with the correct follow-through. The allowances you will therefore have to make will not be consistent.

Potting

Having covered the techniques so far we can now move on to the object of snooker and winning at snooker – potting the balls. So how do you pot the balls you aim for and score points? The answer is by sound judgement – and by remembering where on the object ball you aimed the cue ball when you do pot balls at different angles.

Ask someone who regularly makes a '50 break' how he pots a ball and he will usually say: 'I just hit it.' 'How do you know where to hit it?' The reply comes back: 'I just do.' What he is saying is it's completely by judgement. Potting comes down to natural ability; either you're good at it or you're not.

Needless to say, I must stress that until you can hit the ball consistently in the desired direction, you will never be able to rely on your judgement to pot consistently.

What will help you improve your potting is to learn to recognise potting angles. You must work out what angle you need to strike the object ball with the white before you get down to play the shot. If you try to work out the angle once you are down, it will not be nearly so obvious, since you will not have a total view of the angle of the two balls in relation to the pocket.

The one thing you mustn't do is to think in terms of aiming at a spot on the object ball. Although it is roughly true to say the actual contact point on the object ball will be directly in line with the pocket and the centre of the object ball, it is impossible to aim for this point with any degree of accuracy. In fact, for angled shots the point of contact on the object ball will not be on the same line as that of the cue. If you were to aim for this point with the cue you would hit the object ball fractionally earlier — that is, closer to

you – than expected and not achieve the required direction.

So are there any definite lines of aim for potting shots? Well yes, there are. It is obvious that to hit a ball dead straight requires the white to travel along a path so that when contact is made with the object ball, the white completely covers the ball (looking along the level of the table). This is a full-ball shot. The other extreme is when playing a very fine cut. The path along which the white must travel is such that the extreme outside edge of the white just clips the object ball.

In between you would think there were a million different potting angles. Effectively these can be reduced to three. First of all, the half-ball shot is where the centre of the white is aimed at the extreme

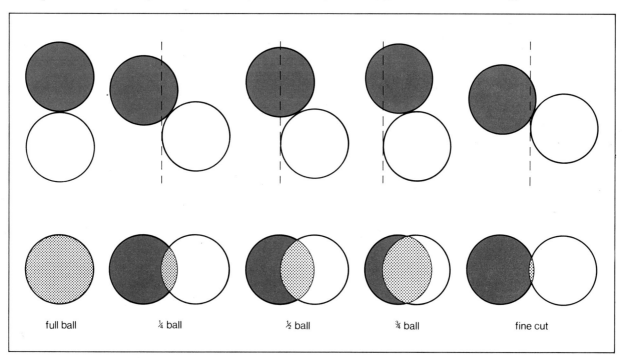

full ball   ¼ ball   ½ ball   ¾ ball   fine cut

Fig. 40 *A bird's eye view shows you the contact you want with the white and the object ball for the five basic shots – full, quarter, half, three-quarter and fine cut. The shaded areas on the player's view of the shots indicate the area of contact for each of the five shots.*

outside edge of the object ball. This is a definite aiming point. After a while you will get to recognise a half-ball shot anywhere on the table.

More judgement is required for the three-quarter-ball shot, but the objective here is to aim the white to cover up three-quarters of the face of the object ball. Similarly with the quarter-ball shot, you must aim to cover a quarter of the face of the object ball.

So this gives you five definite lines of aim (Fig. 40), none of which needs any judgement other than recognition of the angle the two balls make with the pocket. The more you play, the more this will become fixed in your mind. Of course, not every shot will be an exact quarter-, half- or three-quarter-ball, for example. But once you can recognise the basic angles you can adjust to play a thicker or thinner shot as required.

If you do have trouble recognising the angle of the shots, try to imagine the cue ball touching the object ball in such a position as to send the object ball towards the pocket. This is a good guide, although not entirely accurate because there is resistance between the balls and the cloth that makes all angled shots play slightly thicker.

Try also to imagine a corridor along which the cue ball will have to travel to meet the object ball. This then makes potting a ball more like putting one disc on top of another disc. Basically what you are trying to achieve is to cover up a certain proportion (a quarter, half, etc) of the object disc with the other disc.

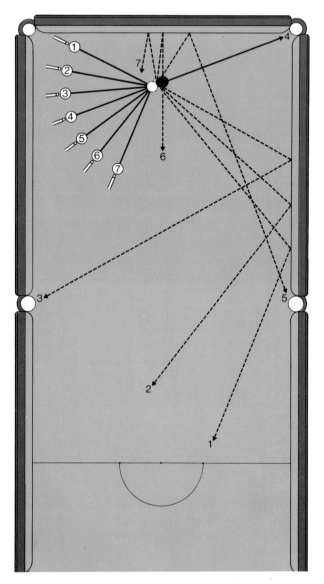

Fig. 41 *Potting the black from different angles: quarter-ball (1), half-ball (2), three-quarter-ball (3), full-ball (4), three-quarter-ball (5), half-ball (6) and quarter-ball (7). The broken lines show the directions the cue ball will travel after contact with the black when playing a plain-ball shot (i.e. without side or screw).*

Hints on practice

Practise potting the black into one of the top pockets from its spot using different angles.

Set up a ring of reds around the black on its spot. Position these by lining them up, judging it so that to pot the ball you would have to cover all the black (full-ball), three-quarters of the black (three-quarter-ball), half the black (half-ball) and quarter of the black (quarter-ball) from each side. You should end up with seven reds in an arc, all roughly the same distance from the black.

If you are allowed, instead of the reds mark their positions with a cross using tailor's chalk. This won't mark the cloth permanently, since it brushes off easily. Make sure you get permission to do this if the table isn't your own.

Working from right to left, try potting the black from all the different positions until you familiarise yourself with these angles.

This is something I used to do for hours on end. Watch where the cue ball goes and where it ends up each time and make a mental note (Figs. 41 to 49).

Do this same practice with blue and pink.

Fig. 42 *Setting up the ring of reds around the black to practise potting it at different angles.*

Fig. 43 *The quarter-ball angle on the black.*

Fig. 45 *The three-quarter-ball angle on the black.*

Fig. 44 *The half-ball angle on the black.*

Fig. 46 *The full-ball angle on the black.*

Fig. 47 *The three-quarter-ball angle on the black.*

Fig. 49 *The quarter-ball angle on the black.*

Fig. 48 *The half-ball angle on the black.*

Chapter 3 **Advanced techniques**

Screw, stun and drag

The screw, stun and drag are all the same shot; each requires the cue ball to be hit below centre. The white is propelled forward, but all the time it is actually rotating backwards. Depending on the stage at which it loses its back spin, you will either make it come back after hitting the object ball (a screw shot), stop dead on contact with the object ball (a stun shot), or drastically slow down in speed before it hits the object ball (a drag shot). With the drag shot, the ball continues to run through after contact, but more slowly than with a plain-ball shot. The difference between the three shots is shown in Fig. 50.

Screw

When you screw back, the white stops for a fraction of a second on contact with the object ball, grips the cloth and enables the back spin to take effect. How far it comes back depends on the distance it has to travel before it hits the object ball and how much back spin combined with power there is in the shot.

Of course this is much harder to play than the plain-ball shot because you are using the edge of the tip to hit the ball. This is the reason why the tip is domed. Because the cue must point slightly downwards, you will be restricted by the height of the cushion and the bridge, so you must try to keep the cue as horizontal as possible.

You can lower the bridge by twisting the hand over slightly or just by flattening it a bit. There is no difference in the way you grip the cue, but you must make sure when altering the bridge that you still have a deep 'V'. A few players prefer to adopt the loop bridge for this shot, but I would not recommend it for the reasons I have already stated.

To illustrate the extra problems with this shot, with regard to playing with unintentional side, try hitting the cue ball up and down the spots as if playing a screw shot. Watch the effect you get. You will find it is much more difficult to keep the white on line.

You can, of course, screw back the white just by

raising the butt of the cue in the air, which a lot of bad players do. But the more you do this, the more you will be hitting into the cloth. This not only limits your follow-through but also invites miscueing, unintentional swerving and also the white leaving the bed of the cloth. This could result in the white still bouncing slightly when hitting the object ball.

The way you strike the ball should be no different from any other shot, although of course it requires more power to screw back two feet than to run through two feet because the momentum of the cue ball has to be stopped before the back spin can take effect.

The cloth has a tendency to dissipate back spin on the cue ball. The further away the white is from the object ball, the more power you require in the shot to keep the back spin on the white.

When you have played the screw shot, once again leave the cue there and concentrate on keeping your head down. There is a particular tendency with this shot to pull the cue back quickly and lift your head up in an effort to avoid the white touching the tip of the cue on the way back. This is a common fault, but the chances of this happening are negligible.

As this shot requires a lot more accuracy of striking than a plain-ball shot, it is important to keep absolutely firm during cue delivery.

The screw shot is probably the most satisfying of all shots to play correctly. Inexperienced players tend to be frightened of playing the shot since they think something special is required to achieve it. I have even been asked if there are special tips for screwing back. The main problem among players not being able to screw back is that they do not strike the cue ball as low as they aim or intend to. It could be they are scared of ripping the cloth (which is very unlikely) or miscueing, or because they lift their head up.

Stun

The stun shot occurs when so much of the back spin has worn off the white as it travels over the cloth that by the time it strikes the object ball there is only

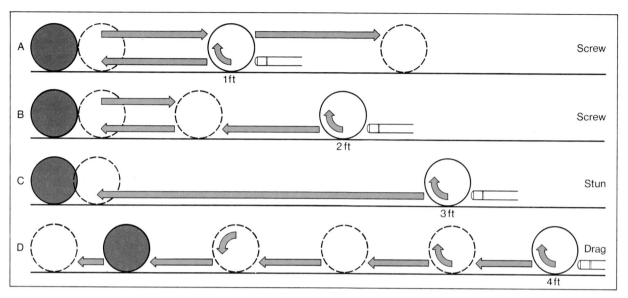

Fig. 50 *shows the difference distance makes when playing a screw shot. Each of the four shots is played with the same strength. In A it is fairly easy to screw back the cue ball beyond its original position because of the short distance between it and the object ball. In B, over a longer distance, there is less screw back. In C there is just enough screw back for the cue ball to stop dead on contact with the object ball. In D, over a much longer distance, the back spin is eventually taken off the cue ball by the cloth and eventually starts rolling forwards.*

enough spin left to stop the white dead.

The great advantage of this shot is that you will know exactly where the white is going to end up. It is therefore useful in positional play. With a screw or drag shot, you can never guarantee exactly where the white will finally come to rest.

The stun with run-through is a very important shot when you need to pot a ball and run the white through just a few inches. Playing this normally would mean trickling the object ball into the pocket. This would invite problems such as the deviation through the nap or the effect of the table not being level. To avoid playing this hazardous shot, use the stun with run-through. If you aim the cue tip on the white slightly above where you would for a stun shot, you will find you can cut out nearly all the forward momentum but still hit the shot firmly.

Drag

When you send the white a long distance before contact with the object ball, but want to play a soft shot, you can just trickle it along. Again you will be faced with the danger of the cue ball deviating on its way to the object ball. This is especially apparent when playing at an angle to the nap.

The drag shot eliminates this, because you are able to hit the white a lot harder; but by the time the white has reached the object ball, it is travelling at the same speed as if you had played a plain ball with no screw back on it.

This is achieved by aiming very low on the white as if to play a screw shot, but making sure when you play the shot that all the back spin has worn off before striking the object ball. You will learn this by trial and error. What it enables you to do is hit the ball much

47

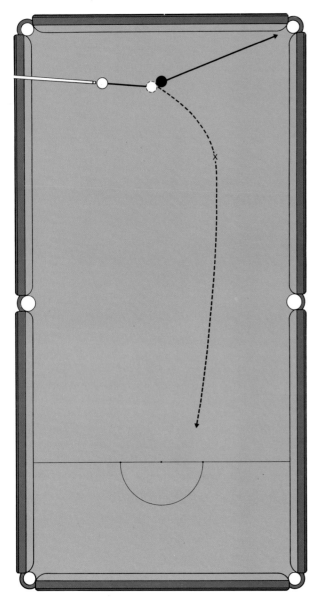

Fig. 51 *The thinner the contact with the object ball, the more the white will travel off-line before the back spin takes effect, resulting in a curve. Point X is where the forward momentum is neutralised by the back spin.*

harder, thus keeping on a true line. As the back spin wears off, the white will slow down, slide over the cloth for a short way, then grip and roll forwards more slowly. In effect, it is like playing the shot from a much shorter distance.

With these three shots, always remember that it is better to screw back accurately than to screw back a long way. So my advice here is don't run before you can walk. Make sure you have complete control over your screw shots before you start to lengthen them.

A further point to bear in mind is that when you play a screw shot for an angled pot, the angle at which the white comes off will be different from a plain-ball shot. I'll try to illustrate this.

If you are playing a full-ball shot with screw back, the white will tend to come back in an absolutely straight line. But the less of the object ball you are covering up, the more the white will tend to travel to one side before the back spin takes effect. This will create a slight curving effect (Fig. 51). The more power you put into a screw shot at an angle, the further off-line the ball will travel before the back spin takes effect. This will create a wider arc. With a stun shot at an angle, the white will come off at a wider angle than for a plain-ball shot with follow-through, but there will be no curve.

Top spin

To put top spin on the ball involves what it suggests – striking the cue ball above centre. The effect you get is to send the white spinning faster than it is actually travelling. Because the ball goes through faster, this enables you to increase the distance of your follow-through after hitting the object ball. This is a much disregarded shot; in fact, extreme top spin is just as difficult to play as screw back. Once again you are using just a small part of the cue tip.

You use top spin to increase the speed at which the white travels through after contact with the object ball. Particularly if you are making a thick contact

Hints on practice

Practise screwing the white back off the blue from varying distances and watch the effect you get.

Put the blue on its spot and the white 12 inches away in line with the middle pocket. Practise first of all stunning the ball dead. Go on to screw back the white a few inches, then 6 inches, then 12 inches, then 1½ feet and then 2 feet, setting marker balls to where you want to screw back. Eventually try to screw back so the white finishes on the lip of the pocket, but doesn't go in.

When you can do this and say it wasn't just luck, you can then claim to have got control of the cue ball.

Put the white 2 feet away from the blue and do the same thing. This gets harder the further away the balls are.

The whole idea is to keep control of the cue ball. It's just as important to be able to run through a set distance, as well.

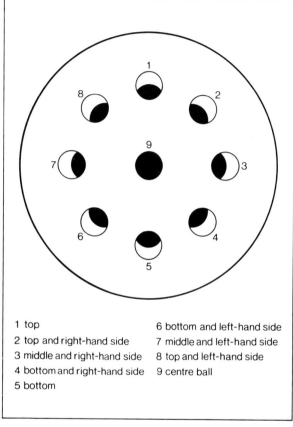

1 top	6 bottom and left-hand side
2 top and right-hand side	7 middle and left-hand side
3 middle and right-hand side	8 top and left-hand side
4 bottom and right-hand side	9 centre ball
5 bottom	

Fig. 52 *The various positions on the cue ball you should aim at for those shots other than centre-ball ones. The shaded areas indicate the amount of the tip that will be in contact with the ball, due to the curved surface. The further to the edge of the ball you aim, the less of the tip will be in contact – and therefore the greater the care needed to prevent miscueing.*

with the object ball, the effect is that the more object ball you hit, the more resistance there is to follow-through; therefore more top spin is required.

Side

If you ever want to become an above average player – to the extent that you can reach the '50 break' milestone – you must be able to play shots with side. Having said that, side can be a dangerous weapon in the wrong hands. It's amazing how many players you see using side for no particular reason. Professionals – and of course I include here good amateurs – only use it when they have to; so don't use it unnecessarily.

The same goes for screw shots, where a plain-ball shot would be just as effective.

Fig. 53 *Hitting the centre of the cue ball – a plain-ball.*

Fig. 54 *Hitting the cue ball with top spin.*

Fig. 55 *Hitting the bottom of the cue ball – screw shot.*

Fig. 56 *Hitting the cue ball with right-hand side.*

Fig. 57 *Hitting the cue ball with left-hand side.*

Fig. 58 *Hitting the cue ball with bottom and right-hand side.*

Fig. 59 *Hitting the cue ball with bottom and left-hand side.*

Fig. 60 *Hitting the cue ball with top and left-hand side.*

Fig. 61 *Hitting the cue ball with top and right-hand side.*

Sometimes it is absolutely necessary to use side to get into a good position for your next shot. But it does make the pot that much harder, especially the further away the white is from the object ball.

Before I talk about side and its uses, I must stress certain points. You must know when you are using side, otherwise you will tend to use it all the time without thinking. And, if you don't know when you are using it, you won't have any control over it. If you do use side, don't make it a substitute for striking the ball in the middle. Make sure you can hit the plain ball accurately and consistently first; then you can practise side shots. Every now and again I deliberately don't use any side at all to make sure I still know what a plain-ball shot is.

Side is used to alter the angle at which the white would normally come off the cushion using a plain-ball shot. This increases, therefore, the range of positions in which you can place the white. The greater the amount of side you are able to put on the ball, the more you can vary the angle at which the white can come off the cushion.

Only by understanding the effects of side – and by a process of trial and error – will you be able to work out where the white is going to end up. It's obvious, but I must still stress it, that if you can't predict roughly where the white is going without side, you have very little chance of playing side constructively and effectively.

There are really no firm guidelines I can give on playing with side. You must find out eventually from experimenting and observing the different effects on the ball. Certain basic principles are worth mentioning, however, Few people realise what happens when the white played with side makes contact with the object ball – or even what path it takes on its way to the object ball.

When you strike the white with side, it will swerve out from the line of the shot slightly before coming back in to make contact with the object ball. This means that both the object ball and the white will go

51

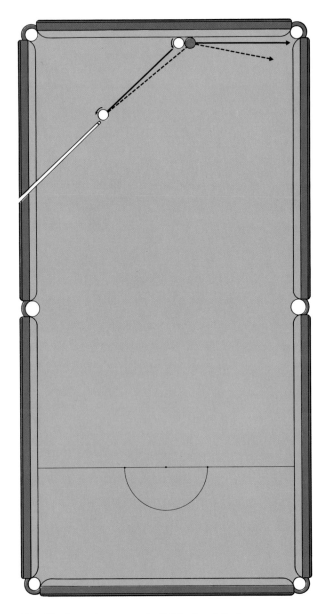

Fig. 62 *shows the correct (solid line) and the incorrect (broken line) shots to play in order to pot a ball along the cushion using side.*

off at a different angle from a plain-ball shot.

If, for example, you play the white with left-hand side, the initial thrust with the cue will push the white slightly to the right before it comes back on course and, in some cases, crosses over the line of the shot. So much, therefore, depends on how much side you put on the white, how hard you strike it, the quality of the cloth, etc. The tip and the type of cue can also affect this, yet another reason for using your own cue.

You will also have to take into consideration how far the object ball is from the white, so the use of side becomes very much trial and error. You will just have to practise it and see what happens. In most cases, it seems as if you have to aim to miss the pot in order to get it.

Another thing happens when the white, struck with side, hits the object ball. The direction the object ball travels after contact is different from that travelled by a plain-ball shot striking the same contact point on the object ball. This might sound very complex, but the following example should help you see what I mean.

Put the black on its spot and the white level, but to the right, of the pink spot to create a half-ball pot on the black into the top left-hand pocket. If you hit the white with right-hand side, the black will tend to be flicked to the left of the pocket. If you attempt the same shot with left-hand side, the black will tend to go to the right of the pocket.

Good players play with side so many times that they don't have to stop to think about it. They will automatically make the necessary adjustments to the angle of the pot. You will have to learn to do the same.

Potting down the cushion with side

When the object ball is resting on a cushion with the white slightly away from the cushion, there is little room for error since the pocket is effectively smaller. This is not the easiest of shots at the best of times, but here is a hint that may increase your chances of success.

Aim the white, using right-hand side, to hit the cushion fractionally earlier than the object ball. Because the side widens the angle at which the white comes off the cushion, the white is on the potting line of the object ball for a little bit longer than it would be with a plain-ball shot (Fig. 62). This means you will marginally increase your chances of sending the object ball along the cushion and into the pocket. This still doesn't make the pot a certainty, but it will make success more likely.

Transmitted side

A lot of players – and that includes top ones – believe, for some reason, that the increased chances of success for the pot along the cushion are due to the fact that side is transmitted from the cue ball on to the object ball and thus helps it into the pocket.

As far as I'm concerned, this is rubbish. I just don't see how this could happen when you've got two perfectly smooth, highly polished surfaces in contact with each other – especially when friction between them is absolutely minimal. For any side to be transmitted, there must be as much friction and contact as there would be between the cue tip and the white.

If I were you, I would ignore the theory altogether. I say there is no such thing as transmitted side.

Screw back with side

This is one of the most advanced shots to play. It involves not only hitting the ball on the bottom but also to one side. Here you must be very accurate with your cueing because you are aiming at such a limited area on the cue ball. As with all shots requiring anything other than centre-ball striking, the better the technique needs to be to master the shot.

After potting a ball normally and running through with side on to the cushion, this shot also gives you a greater range of positions. If you screw a plain-ball shot and the white then hits a cushion, it will bounce off at a particular angle. But if you can master screwing back with side, this will help increase the

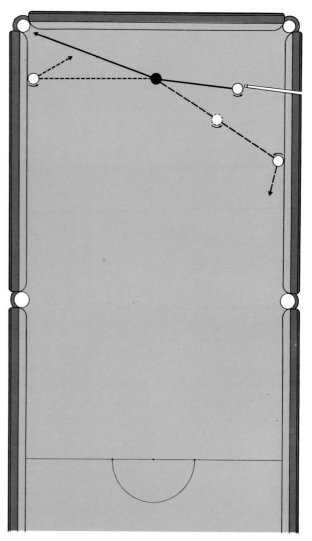

Fig. 63 *Here is a tip to remember when you play a shot with side. With just side, the cue ball will follow through after contact with the object ball and run off the cushion in the same direction as the side you put on it – in this case, right-hand side. If you play the same shot with screw as well, the cue ball will travel off the cushion in the opposite direction (i.e. to the left). This is because the direction of the ball has been changed, although the side remains the same.*

53

range of table open to you for the next shot (Fig. 63).

Of course this shot can only really be played with any effect when the white has to travel over only shortish distances to the object ball – and back – as the side wears off very quickly. And unless the shot is played with extreme side, any effect will have worn off by the time it reaches a cushion so that there will be no noticeably different effect from it.

Power shots

Playing power shots is the one time you may have to make a slight exception to the basic techniques of cue action. You will find it very difficult to keep your head and body perfectly still and not drop the elbow when playing these shots.

Because of the power and longer back swing you need, you won't be able to follow through so far unless you can really thrust the cue a long way forward to generate the extremes of top, screw, side etc. This involves, for the really big power shot, a fair bit of momentum in the body since it seems to be a shot that requires putting your whole self into it. Because you will automatically lift your head up and move the body, there will be a much greater chance of error.

What the beginner thinks is a power shot is not what I would call a power shot. And I'm not talking about a shot that has to be hit hard, since this can be done with absolutely no movement of the body or head. Don't, however, think this is an excuse to start lifting your head on the pretext that you are playing a power shot. I'm talking about a shot that the top players only play if it's absolutely necessary. If there is another shot available, they will have no hesitation in playing that shot in preference.

Once again, the harder you have to hit the ball, the more chance of error. So keep this to a minimum; never play a shot with any more force than is needed. If you watch top players, of course they do play power shots. But the majority of the shots they play are straightforward ones that 'make it look so easy'.

I have developed my power shot gradually. Now I

can screw the ball back a lot better and a lot easier than before I had mastered this type of shot.

If you do want to play a power shot, make sure you keep your head down as much as possible. Brace the body and keep your feet and bridge really firm. The pause before the shot and the general timing are also very important. The tendency otherwise is to snatch at the cue ball, although this is usually a sign of lack of confidence and anxiety.

Swerve

This is a shot you must learn to master. It's surprising how many people don't know how to play it. But it is essential for getting out of snookers without the problems of judging angles off the cushions.

To play a swerve shot, you have to hit down on the white with either left- or right-hand side, depending on the direction you want to bend the ball. To some extent you can bend the ball just with side and perhaps a little bit of screw. But the distance you can make the ball deviate will be minimal. What you are

Fig. 64 *When playing the swerve shot – for example, to get out of a snooker – you need to hit down on the cue ball with side to create the maximum swerving effect.*

54

doing when you play a proper swerve shot is, by hitting down on the ball, making it bounce very slightly. And only when the ball stops bouncing, can it grip the cloth and start to move off-line. It is, in a way, similar to the effect a spin bowler can get with a cricket ball.

How you play this shot accurately is, again, a matter of judgement. You must aim to miss the ball you want to get round. The white will then bounce outside the line of that ball, grip the cloth and, with the side taking effect, cut back in to hit the object ball. Accuracy, however, will only come with lots of practice and once again no panic in the cue action.

The severity and distance of the swerve will depend on the amount of side you put on the white and the speed at which the shot is played. The harder you play the shot, the longer the distance of the swerve but the less severely it is liable to cut back, because there is more bounce on the ball. The greater the arc you want, the more you should concentrate on hitting the ball with extreme side to make the ball really bite. Going back to the analogy with cricket, it is much more difficult for a fast bowler to spin the ball than for a slow bowler.

The grip you get on the cloth is very important and this will partly depend on the quality of the cloth. The newer it is, the more grip you will get. Make sure, also, that you strike the white crisply.

A quick reminder here about how side works. Left-hand side will push the white out to the right and then back in again – and vice-versa with right-hand side. Also the steeper the cue action, usually the more swerve you will achieve.

The rest

The rest is an extension of your bridge and should be used when you cannot reach across the table comfortably to play a shot. Never overstretch or try to play with too long a bridge or you will lose control over the cue.

How far you can reach before you need to use a rest will, of course, depend on your height and how

Fig. 65 *When playing with the rest, you must still get your head as low down over the shot as you can and line up the shot in the normal way.*

55

Fig. 66 *Using the rest. Notice how the feet are positioned to give you a solid stance.*

Fig. 67 *When using the rest, keep as much of the left forearm as possible on the table for extra support.*

long your arms are. From the baulk end of the table I can comfortably reach to play the white from just before the blue spot without a rest, although admittedly I am bridging a little bit longer than average.

You often find players overstretching when they cue up because they are afraid to use the rest. Don't be. Always make a point of using the rest when it is needed. If you get into the bad habit of avoiding it, you will never get into the habit of using it correctly when you really need it.

You should have the head of the rest roughly the same distance from the white as your bridge would be – possibly slightly further away. The rest is, of course, a fixed height from the cloth. You will notice the head of the rest is made up of a high 'X' and a low 'X'. I nearly always use the low 'X', which is a fraction higher than my bridged hand would be, and position it back a bit from the normal bridge length position.

There is a theory about using the high 'X' for getting on top of the white and the low 'X' for playing screw shots, for example, where you need to hit below the centre of the ball. I very rarely use the high 'X' except when I want a power follow-through, since I find the low 'X' is in most cases suitable for all types of shot. You must still try to keep the cue as horizontal as possible, although the actual bridge is higher than your hand would be. The low 'X' helps you do this more than the high 'X'.

Hold the rest securely and keep the butt end firmly on the table. You must make sure the head of the rest is immovable. As you get down, make sure your head is as low as possible in line with the shot without being uncomfortable. Try to ensure you can still get in a rifle-sighting position.

Probably one of the reasons people find the rest shots harder to play is because of the altered arm action. This is a sideways motion of the right arm. The elbow starts off almost at right angles to the cue and comes in as the arm straightens out when you play the shot. It is important to keep this arm horizontal to the ground or table. Apart from this, the cueing action is the same as normal, with back swing, pause and follow-through.

If I had the choice of playing a shot with or without the rest, I would chose the latter. But I still made sure I conquered it to the extent that now it never frightens me when I have to use it.

You are, of course, limited in the range of shots you can play with any confidence using the rest. But as long as you are not too adventurous with it, you should, with practice, develop a fair amount of accuracy.

The long rest

The long rest and cue are big and cumbersome and here you should definitely never attempt anything too adventurous with them. When you have to use them, make sure you only play plain-ball shots. Keep the action as smooth as possible and just stroke the cue ball on to the object ball.

The longer cue has a bigger and thicker tip on the end. Therefore with any attempt at screw-back or side, for example, the effect is reduced by the fact that the thicker the tip, the nearer the centre of the ball you will be hitting.

You should not have much need for this rest, anyway. I rarely use it because, fortunately, with the normal rest I can reach the white just before the pink spot from the baulk end of the table.

The spider

Everybody hates using the spider to bridge over intervening balls since it is hard enough bridging normally over them.

The main disadvantage of the spider is that you have to play the shot from up in the air, hitting down over the ball. This means any side you put on the white will be exaggerated. Try as far as possible to concentrate hitting the white in the centre – and not hard. There is a tendency with this type of shot to jerk or snatch at it. I have already warned of the dangers of doing this. Make sure you play the shot with a good, smooth action or you are quite likely to mis-cue.

In most cases you will be using the spider around the pack of reds, probably trying to pot a red into a top corner pocket to keep on the black. Therefore the fact that all you can do is roll the red into the pocket and not play any advanced shots is no real handicap. In this case there is usually little distance between the white, the object ball and the pocket. When there is any great distance between the cue ball and the object ball, accuracy is virtually impossible.

Chapter 4 Planning

Positional play

After the basic techniques, this is the most important part of the game of snooker, incorporating at some time or another all the advanced shots I have mentioned. When – and only when – you no longer have to concentrate on striking the ball and potting accurately and consistently, can you devote your mind to controlling the cue ball, which of course is the essence of positional play.

There are no short cuts. The best way to learn about positioning is by trial and error, which involves watching where the cue ball goes after each type of shot you play. When practising different shots, make a note of where the white ends up and each time try to change its course by adjusting the type of shot you play. Then see if you can predict where it will go when you play a certain shot. When you can do this every time, you should be able to look forward to plenty of high breaks. But it's much harder in practice than I have made it sound, to the extent that even I am still learning.

I could illustrate numerous examples of the positional shots you can play, because there are always so many possibilities. In the end, it's up to you to work out the shots for yourself.

I personally found that billiards taught me a great deal about positioning. I would certainly recommend it as a means of initial practice, because the emphasis is much more on cue ball control than even in snooker in some cases.

Most people tend to think that the top professionals and amateurs play to put the cue ball on a sixpence. But this is a fallacy. They usually play what we call 'percentage positioning', which means giving themselves as big an area as possible in which to put the cue ball to get them comfortably on the next shot. This means that they can allow for the greatest margin of error possible, should things not go quite as planned.

There are, of course, occasionally shots where accurate positioning of the cue ball is critical; but these are fewer than you would probably think. Every shot in snooker offers a new challenge since the balls are rarely in the same position. That's what makes it such an absorbing game.

While I am on this point, it's worth looking at another question I am sometimes asked: 'How many balls ahead do the professionals think? Surprisingly enough, the answer is not very many. It's not like a game of chess, although of course you size up the state of the table and work out how much is 'on' and whether, for example, you can see a big break there. Usually the top player may be thinking at most three or four balls ahead. To take any greater amount of concentration off the shot in hand would be wrong. It's more a case of reading the table and knowing where the pitfalls are, and this comes after years of practice.

Planning more shots ahead than that is not usually necessary anyway. The type of shot the good player makes should allow him several alternatives. This way he can get out of trouble and back on course within the space of a very few shots. From experience you tend to know automatically how you hope to put a break together and you gradually work your way towards it.

This also incorporates tactics. One useful tip for very big breaks is to reposition any awkward balls, such as those lying up against the cushion or touching another ball. This can be done by cannoning on to them from a previous shot. But make sure that even if you don't put the awkward ball into a good potting position, you are still on to pot another ball.

You can use this tactic to good effect, particularly when there are plenty of reds on the table. In effect you are setting them up for when you will need to play them. You don't want to be on a large break with the last remaining red in an unpottable position, when you could at an early stage have cannoned it into the middle of the table.

Playing cannons at billiards, incidentally, is of great help in getting to know in what direction the cue

59

ball goes after contact with the object ball.

Avoid the danger areas. For example, don't leave yourself near a cushion – unless, of course, you want to pot along it. Near the cushion you are limiting the range of positional shots you can play. Also avoid having to play pin-point positional shots. Not only will these demand a much higher degree of accuracy, but they make you more prone to ending a break prematurely.

The golden rule is to keep out of trouble as far as is possible. Your opponent may well be doing his best to get you in it, so you don't want to help him by repeatedly messing up the chance of a good break. The higher the level of play, the fewer chances you get anyway.

There is another tip to increase your chance of a big break. Whenever a realistic opportunity arises early on in the game, try to break up the pack of reds. This is mostly done by cannoning into them after potting the black. But make sure you pot the black, otherwise you'll just be letting in your opponent.

Angles

Positional play revolves to a great degree around angles, because you will need to use these to get from the object ball into position for the next shot. So here it is worth making some observations about angles and how they can work.

For a start, certain potting angles are easier to get position off than others. If you are playing a very thick or a very thin contact, you immediately restrict the angle at which the white can come off the object ball. With a full-ball shot, the white is limited to being positioned on the line of the shot whether you screw back or follow through. With a thin cut, the line the white takes afterwards is also predetermined.

It is generally best to aim for a position in which you are playing either a half- or a three-quarter-ball pot, especially the latter since there are probably more positional permutations from this than from any other potting angle (Figs. 68 to 73). It is interesting

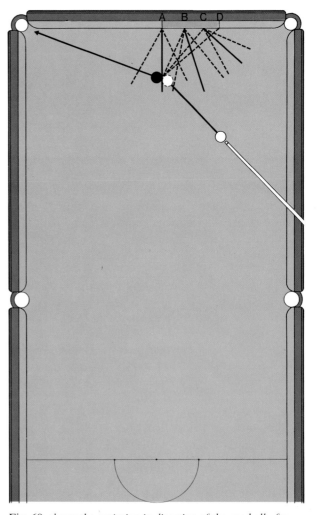

Fig. 68 *shows the variation in direction of the cue ball after a half-ball contact with the black. Point A is the furthest to the left you can hit the cushion; where it goes from there depends on whether you play a plain ball or one with side. The lines to the left and right indicate the directions when using maximum left-hand and right-hand side respectively. The centre line indicates the direction of a plain ball. Point B relates to a stun shot, point C to a screw shot and point D to a shot with maximum screw. As you can see, the area of cushion (shaded area) which can be hit by the cue ball is more limited than when playing a three-quarter ball (Fig. 69).*

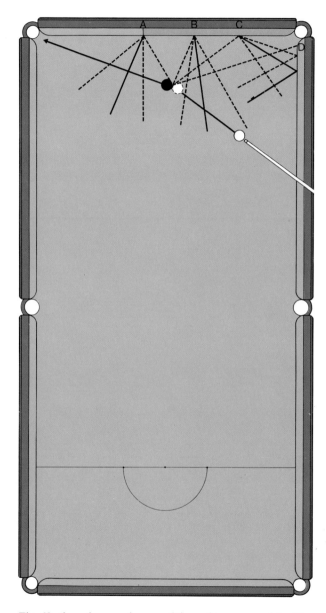

Fig. 69 *shows how much more of the cushion you can hit with the cue after a three-quarter-ball contact with the black. Although you have to play certain shots with more strength than for a half-ball, there is more scope for position.*

to note that with a half-ball pot with plain-ball striking, the white comes off at the widest angle possible. This is unless you start to hit with any force, which tends to widen the angle even further. If you play a plain half-ball shot, not only is the angle at which the object ball comes off guaranteed, but so is the angle of the white.

So after a while, as long as you practise regularly, you should be able to recognise each shot and predict where the cue ball will end up.

Try, whenever possible, to let the white go in the direction it wants to, that is a plain-ball shot. This is the simplest type of shot to play and involves the least risk. The problems start when you try to make the white go in a different direction. Of course you have to play according to the state of the balls. But if there is ever a choice, always go for the easier shot.

One point, very obvious when stated but nevertheless lost on some players, is to make sure you are the right side of your next ball, so you can get position for the shot after that. For example, it's much easier to get on to the reds next shot if you are just below the blue when potting it, than to be above it and have to play the cue ball in and out of baulk.

This is the most important part of all positional play. As long as you are in a position to send the white towards your next object ball and not away from it, you are making life much easier. So always try to think that little bit ahead.

Hints on practice

Red and black potting
Scatter three or four reds around the black – on its spot – and practise potting a red, then black, another red, then black again, until all the reds have gone. Again this will help your positional play.

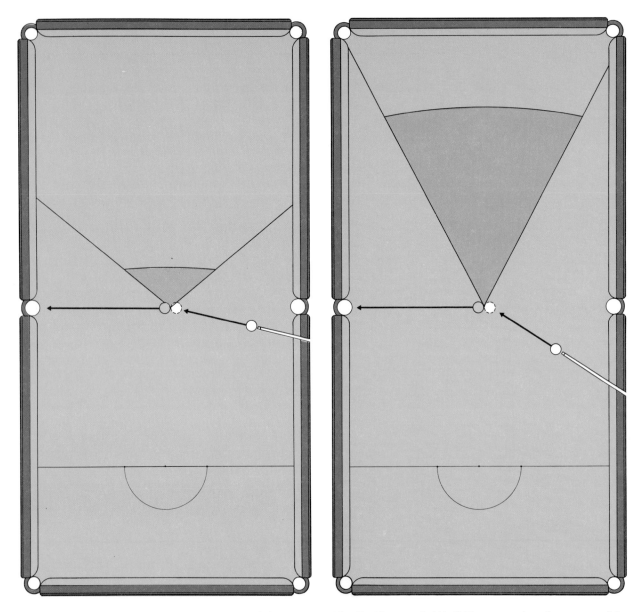

Fig. 70 *Playing a three-quarter-ball blue. The shaded area is that part of the table out of bounds for the cue ball, unless you let it run off the cushion, which would immediately open up more of the table for your cue ball.*

Fig. 71 *Playing a half-ball blue, you reduce the amount of the top of the table in which you can put the cue ball. The ball will also travel further – which can be an advantage if you want to get it back down the table.*

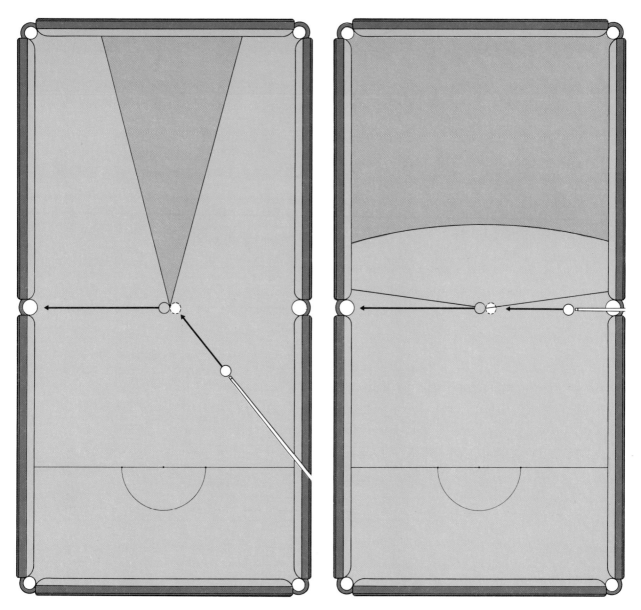

Fig. 72 *Playing a quarter-ball blue, you are even more restricted and it is impossible to stop the cue ball before striking the top cushion. Not the best shot if you want to stay in the top half of the table.*

Fig. 73 *When your angle on the blue is thicker than a three-quarter ball, it becomes increasingly difficult to run the cue ball into the top half of the table without using a cushion.*

Hints on practice

Potting the colours

This exercise enables you to gauge what progress you have made with your game and how consistently you can pot balls and build up a reasonable break.

Put the colours on their spots and try potting them in turn. You can start off with the white in any position. When you have potted the pink, replace all the colours before going for the black.

After potting the black, try to get back in position for the yellow and work your way through the colours again. See how many times you can do this.

Since the object balls are always in a fixed position (on their spots), try to remember which shots that you play bring the best results in terms of gaining position for the next colour.

Potting the black

This is a useful way of practising the different kinds of shot on the black and learning to judge what effects each will have in terms of getting the object ball in the pocket.

Put the black on its spot and try potting it with varying amounts of screw and side. Also vary the distance between the white and the black. Make a note of the allowance that has to be made for the different amounts of side you put on.

Then set yourself an area into which to play the white and practise getting it as close as you can.

Introduce a third ball anywhere on the table and practise playing a cannon off the black on to the second object ball.

Lining up the reds

This exercise demands a reasonable standard before it can be used with any real benefit, but again it will help your positional play and get you used to the pressures and problems of building a big break

With all the colours on their respective spots, position the 15 reds in between the brown-to-black line of colours. Start by potting a red, then a colour, then another red and a colour again. The bigger the break, the harder it gets. Keep a tally of your highest break and then see if you can beat it.

If you feel you don't want the reds all lined up the middle, put them in harder positions around the table.

Combination shots

These involve any type of shot where one object ball is hit on to another ball or balls for a pot to be made. The main type of combination shot is the plant (or set).

The plant

This is when two reds are in such a position that by hitting the first with the white you can pot the second or by hitting the first with the white you can use the second to help the first in. This shot can only be played with any consistent degree of accuracy when the two reds are touching, although the reds don't have to be touching for the shot to be played.

If you have two reds touching and the centre of both balls is lined up with the pocket, you would think that all you had to do was to hit the first and the second could not fail to go in. In practice, strange things happen depending on your aim point on the first red.

The reason for the effects shown in Figs. 74 to 76 is that even though the balls are touching, if you don't aim as if to pot the first red, the second will not go in. This is because in the very short space of time the reds are together, due to the small amount of friction, the first red will push the second just enough to send it off-line. Of course this can work to your advantage if the plant is not exactly lined up for the pocket.

Aiming becomes slightly harder when the two reds are not touching. A tip here that may help you work out where to hit the first red is where on the second red you must hit to send it into the pocket. Line up through the first red to the cushion. The aim for the white on to the first red is to send it on to an imaginary place on the cushion.

Try to strike the first red on to that spot on the cushion. That way, if your judgement is correct, it should hit the second red in the right spot to pot it. Again it is only with practice that you will be able to work out the angles at which the different balls come off after contact.

Take a plant, with the two reds touching but parallel to the pocket. You want to pot the first red, but possibly you are well off the line of the shot. Once again it's not just a question of hitting the first red. You must make sure that the centre of the two reds makes a right angle with the angle of the pot. Secondly you must make sure you do not hit the first red too thick. If you do, the momentum of the white will affect the intended direction of the first red by interfering with the contact between the two reds. Therefore you must still play no more than a half-ball – or thinner – contact to stop the white from interfering and preventing the pot.

My advice is to play these shots in as many different situations as you can and keep an eye on what happens. You'll be surprised at what the balls actually do.

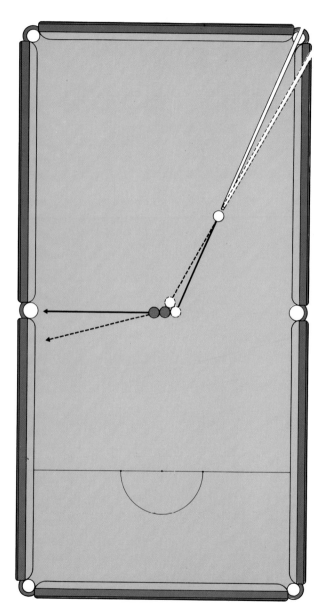

Fig. 74 *Potting a red that forms a plant with another red in line with the pocket. The broken line shows the exaggerated effect of not playing the shot correctly.*

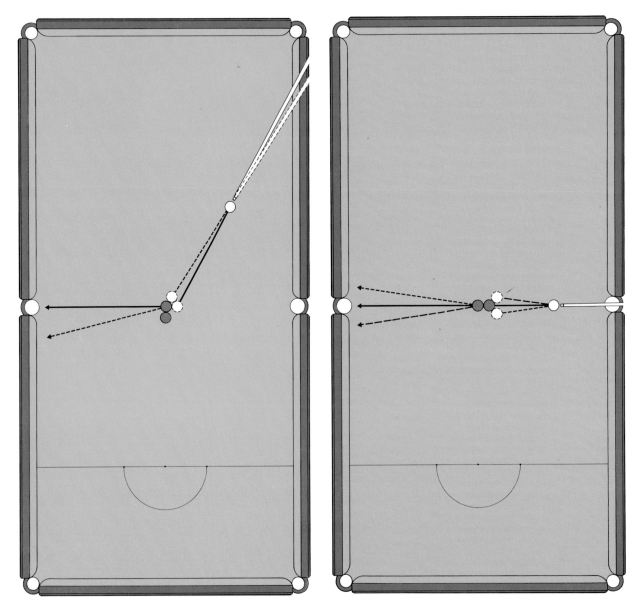

Fig. 75 *Potting a red that forms a plant with another red parallel to the pocket. Again the broken line shows the exaggerated effect of not playing the shot correctly.*

Fig. 76 *Playing a full-ball shot to pot a red that forms a plant with another red, when both are touching and in line with the pocket. The broken lines are the wrong shots.*

The double

It's a common belief that top players don't play doubles. This isn't true; in fact, I once played a treble (using two cushions) to win a match. They certainly don't play them that often, however. Despite that, you should know how to play them all the same, even if you don't use them too often.

There is an element of risk in this shot, because you are dependent on how the cushion is playing. It is for this reason mainly that the better players avoid, where possible, getting themselves in a position where they have to play a double.

A lot of people think that if you hit the ball on to the cushion it will come off at exactly the same angle as it went on. But it doesn't work like that at all. The harder you hit the ball into the cushion, the more it buries itself in and the straighter (or squarer) the cushion releases it. For a ball to come off at the same angle, very little pace is required.

Even so, the angle the ball comes off varies from table to table depending on the state of the rubber in the cushion. It takes several attempts for even a top player to find out exactly how the cushion is playing and how he should play the double.

There are four types of double you can play, which will be made clearer by looking at Figs. 77 to 80. Apart from the ordinary full-ball double, there is the cross double, when the cue ball crosses over the face of the object ball before the latter moves off in the intended direction. There is also the cut-back double – the opposite of this – where the cue ball strikes the far side of the object ball. The hardest double to play is the 'cocked hat' double, where you in fact play the object ball off three cushions (Fig. 80). You will not see this shot played very often, for obvious reasons.

There are no guidelines as to how to play these doubles, except once again by trial and error, getting to know the different reactions at certain speeds of playing the shot. A ball tight on the cushion usually creates more problems than a ball not touching, since it generally becomes harder to visualise the angle

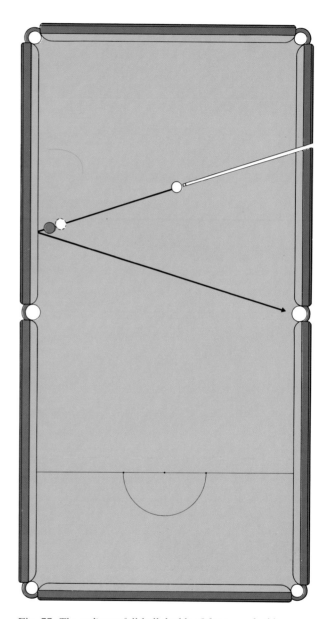

Fig. 77 *The ordinary full-ball double. Of course, doubling into a corner pocket is slightly more difficult since you have less of the pocket to aim at than for a shot into a middle pocket.*

67

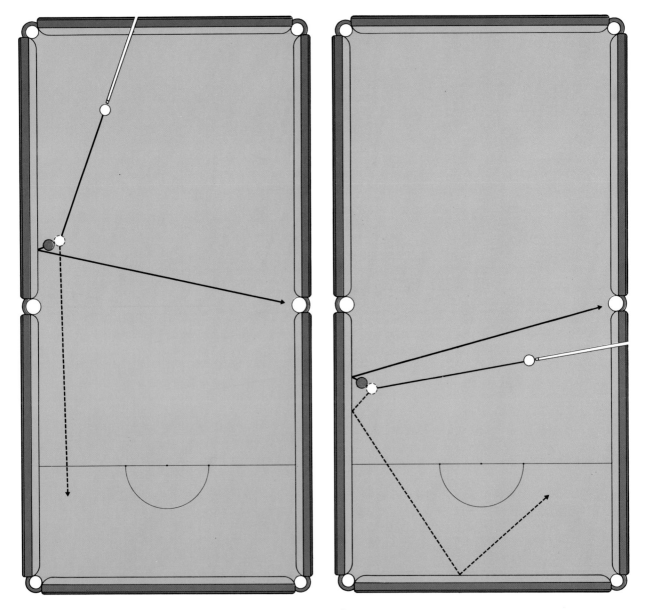

Fig. 78 *The cross double.*

Fig. 79 *The cut-back double.*

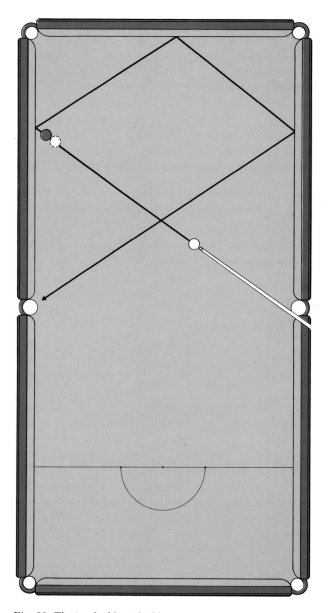

Fig. 80 *The 'cocked hat' double.*

required and it is more likely that the white can interfere with the shot.

A treble is just an extension of this technique. Of course, you are increasing the margin of error, because you have to take into account the effect off two cushions rather than just one.

50 breaks

The first 50 break is a bit of a milestone in every snooker player's life. To achieve it requires a high degree of accuracy and consistency and an overall standard of play you will only reach by dedication and practice.

The following two breaks were played with the colours and four reds left on the table. The point of this section is to illustrate that for any break of this size you will need to play a variety of different shots. It also shows that the course of the break is in no way predetermined. At any stage I could have played them a different way – more so with the first one. Positional play, as I have already said, is about percentage shots – giving yourself as much choice as possible in case you don't play exactly the shot you originally wanted. Follow the diagrams to see how each break went (See Figs. 81 to 111).

First break

My position on red 1 meant I had a thickish three-quarter-ball pot into the top left-hand pocket. I hit the white just off-centre, stunning it to leave me in position on the black. I was intending to get a position off the black to be able to pot red 3 and get back on the black for the next shot. As it was, the white ran further than I wanted and I left myself level with the black and on the wrong side of it to get on to red 3. This meant changing my mind about the next red to go for.

The black was roughly a three-quarter-ball pot into the top left-hand pocket and it meant I could play a plain-ball shot with normal run-through to leave myself on red 2. I potted the black and the white

69

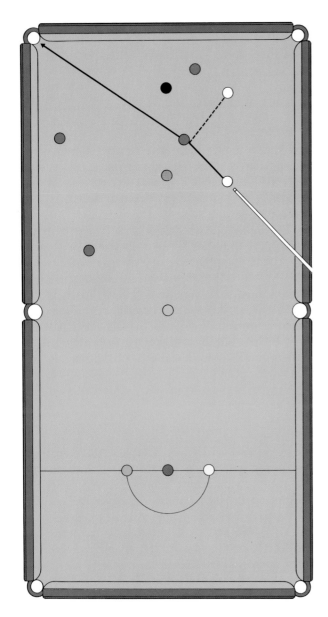

Fig. 81 *Potting red 1. Black is the next shot.*

ran off the side cushion, ending virtually in line with red 2 and the top left-hand pocket. This was all right, except I couldn't play position on the black again. I was stretching slightly for this shot, but I was still comfortable, and had then to decide how far to screw the white down the table. I decided to make sure I screwed back at least as far as straight on the pink, since I didn't want an angle on the pink that meant me going 'away' from the last two reds. I knew that if I screwed back too far I would still be on the blue, thus covering myself.

I potted red 2 and fortunately just avoided being in line with the pink and red 4, which would have meant an awkward shot over red 4 at the pink. Had that happened, I would probably have elected to take the blue. As it was, I was left just off straight for the pink into the top right-hand pocket.

At this stage I had a choice of playing the pink with stun to leave myself in position for red 4 into the middle left-hand pocket, or of rolling the white through, off the side cushion, into position to pot red 3 into the top left-hand pocket. I chose to play position on red 3 because the angle looked perfect and I had a natural shot, without needing to use any side.

It would have been safer to stun the white for position on red 4, because there was less chance of positional error. But I also bore in mind the fact that I had earlier failed to get position on red 3 and by going for red 4 I might have had problems getting back on to red 3 with my next shot. Using top, I potted the pink into the top right-hand pocket and ran through into a perfect angle for red 3, although closer than I would have liked. If I had been any closer, I would have had an awkward shot to play. But it was just as important to be off the cushion.

I was left a thick three-quarter-ball pot, which meant a soft stun to get position on the black for a pot into the same pocket. The one place I didn't want to leave the white was straight on the black, since this would have meant screwing back with side off the cushion – a much more difficult shot than any other

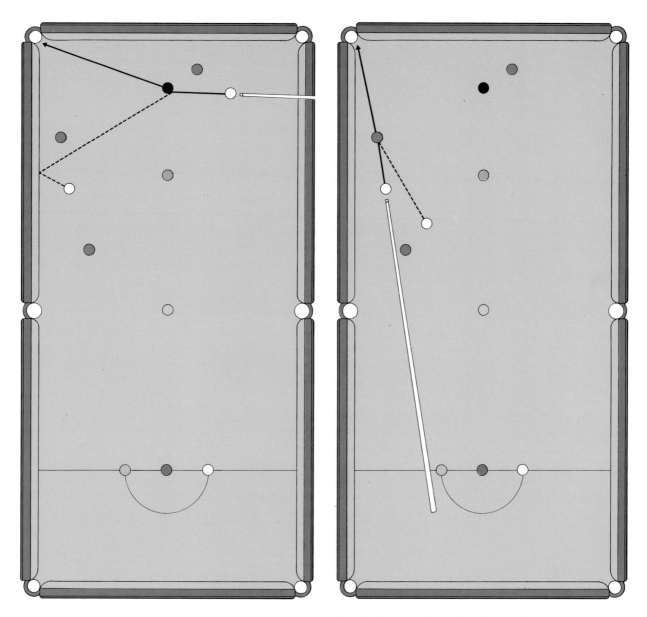

Fig. 82 *Potting black. Red 2 is the next shot.*

Fig. 83 *Potting red 2. Pink is the next shot.*

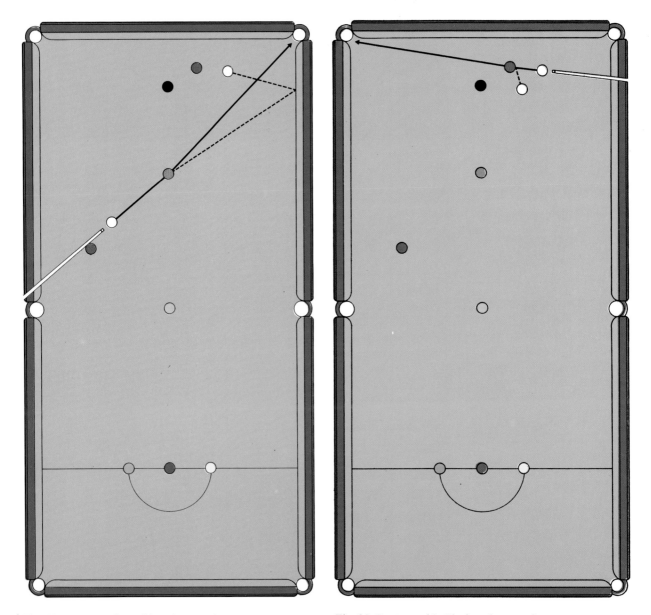

Fig. 84 *Potting pink. Red 3 is the next shot.*

Fig. 85 *Potting red 3. Black is the next shot.*

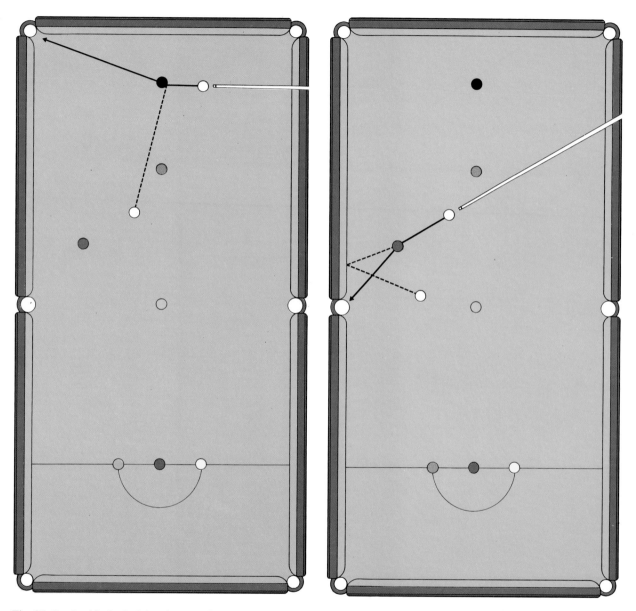

Fig. 86 *Potting black. Red 4 is the next shot.*

Fig. 87 *Potting red 4. Blue is the next shot.*

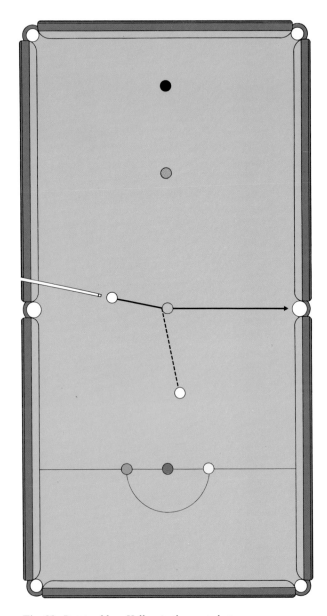

Fig. 88 *Potting blue. Yellow is the next shot.*

here – and also with the chance of the pink interfering with my next shot on to red 4. I potted red 3 and left myself slightly short of straight with the black. Playing with stun I decided to send the white past the pink and towards red 4 to pot that into the middle left-hand pocket.

In potting the black into the top left-hand pocket, I played the shot a little too firmly. Although I was in a good position (thick half-ball) on the final red, it was on the wrong side to roll up naturally for the blue. I could still get on the blue, although the easiest shot would have been to run the white off the side cushion and back on to the pink. It wasn't a difficult shot, either, to screw back for position on the black. However my next ball was yellow, so I was looking for the easiest of the blue, pink and black to get position on this colour for my next shot. Of the three, the blue is the best ball, mainly because it is closest to the yellow.

So I elected to get position on the blue. I potted red 4 using left-hand side, which required a bit more accuracy of striking than a plain-ball shot. I ran through off the cushion in perfect position for a three-quarter-ball shot on the blue.

Playing this with stun I decided to send the white down towards the yellow, hoping to leave myself an angle on the yellow to pot this, bounce off the right-hand side cushion and into position for the green. I potted the blue, but played the shot badly. I didn't hit low enough on the white, which therefore came off a lot less square from the blue than I had wanted. It ended up to the right of the line I wanted. This shot would have been no trouble for a left-hander; but I had to use the rest. Obviously this shot was a lot more difficult to play since I had to run the white off the bottom cushion and back into the middle of the table to get on the green. The danger here was not striking the ball firmly enough and snookering myself on the brown.

I potted the yellow and left myself another three-quarter-ball pot on the green into the bottom left-hand pocket. Perfect! I played a stun shot, sending the

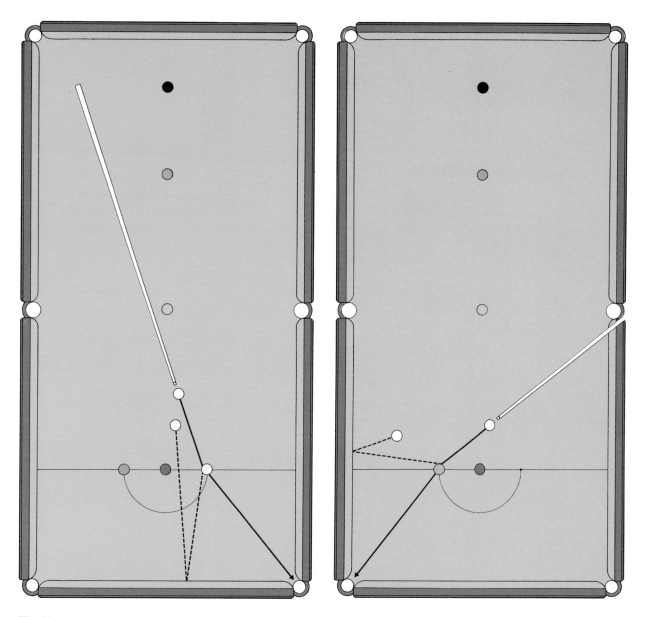

Fig. 89 *Potting yellow. Green is the next shot.*

Fig. 90 *Potting green. Brown is the next shot.*

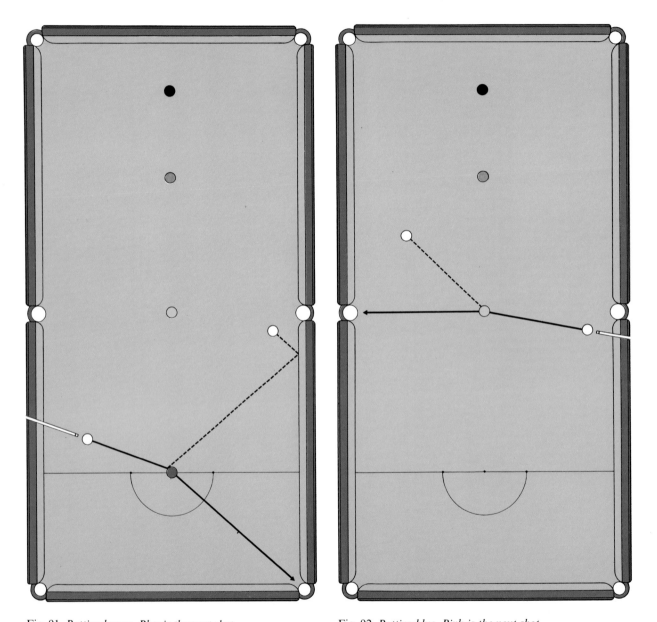

Fig. 91 *Potting brown. Blue is the next shot.*

Fig. 92 *Potting blue. Pink is the next shot.*

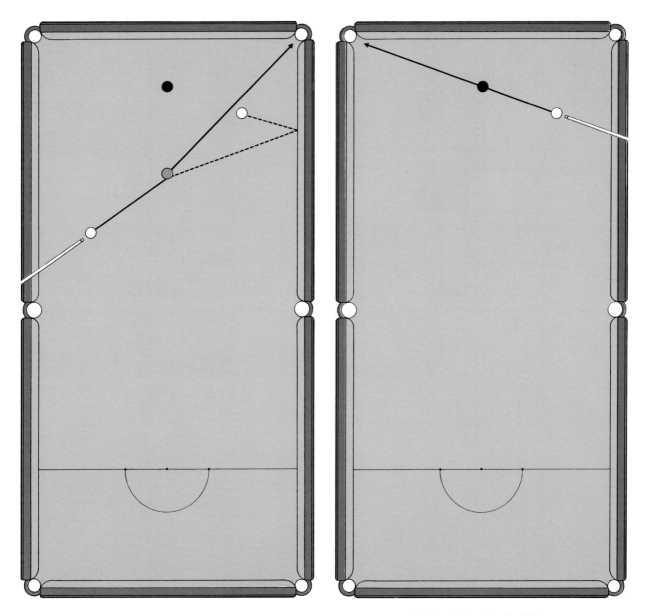

Fig. 93 *Potting pink. Black is the next shot.*

Fig. 94 *Potting black. That's a break of 56.*

white off the side cushion and back on to the brown. Another three-quarter-ball stun saw the white bounce off the side cushion and back up the table for position on the blue. The brown to the blue can be the most important shot when clearing the colours, since perfect position on the blue almost guarantees pink and black. But a bad position on the blue can create problems. When playing the brown, ideally you want to leave the white just below the blue so the natural angle will send the white towards the pink.

Fortunately I was left in perfect position for a three-quarter-ball pot on the blue into the middle left-hand pocket, running the white naturally through on to the pink. This I potted into the top right-hand pocket and ran through off the side cushion. I made sure I was away from the cushion to leave a full-ball pot on the black into the top left-hand pocket. This I stunned in to make sure there was no chance of following through into the same pocket. This completed a break of 56.

Summary

You will notice that all the shots I played in this break were between three-quarter and full-ball contacts with one exception. This is a fairly rare occurence; for various reasons, you don't always want to leave yourself this kind of situation.

These angles are, however, much easier to judge than the half- or quarter-ball ones. There is less problem visualising the white superimposed on the object ball, particularly when it will be covering up a large proportion of the object ball. Try where possible to leave yourself three-quarter balls; they are easier to play since you seem to have more control over the white.

You will notice I only once used side in the whole break; this minimised the chance of error.

It should be clear from this break that you do not need pin-point accuracy in positional play. In fact, there was only one shot that needed any real degree of accurate positioning – and that was when I wanted position on red 3. Of course the strength of my shots was accurate. This plays just as important a part in positioning as does direction.

Second break

This break was set up in such a way that it was going to be much harder to clear the table and, in contrast to the first break, did require precision shots. These I visualised before I started. In the first break, the balls were in easier, more comfortable positions. From the diagrams you can see that there are two difficult reds, the one on the bottom cushion and the one touching the black. The green was off its spot, which meant I would have to get a good position off the yellow to get on the green when it came to pot the colours.

I had to use red 1 to get a good position on a colour and then on the awkward red 2. I had a thick three-quarter-ball pot which I played with stun to put red 1 in the middle right-hand pocket and leave myself on the brown. I had to make sure I didn't leave myself straight on the brown; I wanted roughly a three-quarter ball to get down to red 2 on the left-hand side of the table. The white ended up quite nicely and, with my leg on the table, I could reach it comfortably.

From brown to red 2 was critical. With the red so close to the cushion, the position I needed not only to pot it but also to get on to a colour for the next shot had to be within a limited angle. I was looking for no thicker than a three-quarter and no thinner than a half-ball shot on red 2. So I played a type of stun run-through shot on the brown into the bottom right-hand pocket, allowing the white to run towards the red; it was just a touch shot. I needed to be as close as possible to the red so there was more chance of an accurate contact.

As it turned out I played the brown perfectly and left myself a thickish half-ball shot on red 2. Now I had to think about getting on a colour, since I had a tough shot along the cushion. I wanted to play a reasonably paced shot so the red would not run off course. The nap would tend to take a soft shot away

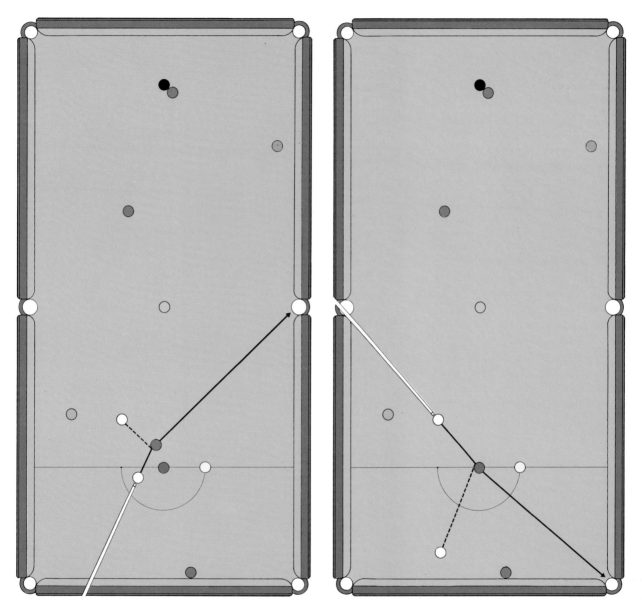

Fig. 95 *Potting red 1. Brown is the next shot.*

Fig. 96 *Potting brown. Red 2 is the next shot.*

from the pocket. If I had played a centre-ball shot at the speed I wanted, the white would have ended up on the side cushion. So I had to play with a bit of left-hand side, which made the shot even harder.

I successfully potted the red into the bottom right-hand pocket and left myself dead straight on the brown. This was not the best place for getting on the next red, but at least I had potted red 2.

Now I had to think in terms of using the next red to get position on probably the blue, which would enable me to cannon the last red away from the black. But first I had to pot the brown and get position on red 3. For this I had to play a power screw shot off the side cushion. The white was 2½ feet away from the brown to start with and I wanted to screw back about 6 feet. Great accuracy was therefore needed. Brown went into the bottom right-hand pocket and I left myself a thick half-ball pot on red 3 into the top left-hand pocket.

With this shot I had to get the white back down the table below the blue so I could then have a chance of getting on the last red, which as I have said had to be separated from the black. I potted red 3 using stun and lots of left-hand side, bringing the white off the side cushion and down below the blue. Because the white speeds up slightly when played with side off a cushion, the weight of the shot had to be more accurate than usual. It would have been easier to judge this using only screw, but the middle pocket was in the way.

As it was, the shot was perfect and I left myself a half-ball pot on the blue, the ideal angle to attempt to get red 4 out into play. This shot also demanded a high degree of accuracy. But there was also a large element of luck involved, since even if I did get the cannon on the black and red, I still couldn't guarantee the two balls would split up favourably.

I stunned the blue into the middle right-hand pocket. Ideally I was looking to hit the red on the left-hand side just before hitting the black, since this would have sent the red bouncing off the cushion

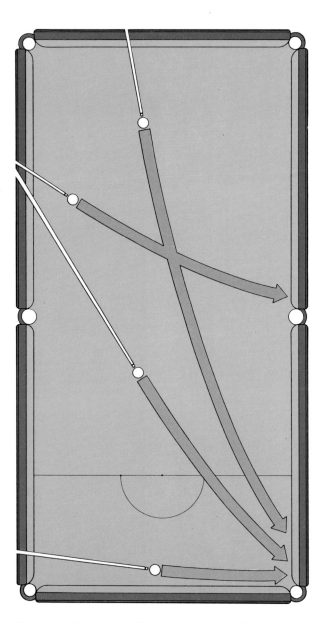

Figs. 97 to 99 *show the effect that the nap, which runs from the baulk end to the top of the table, can have on the ball. When playing against the nap, the cue ball is going 'uphill' against the cloth and the effect is to carry the ball away from*

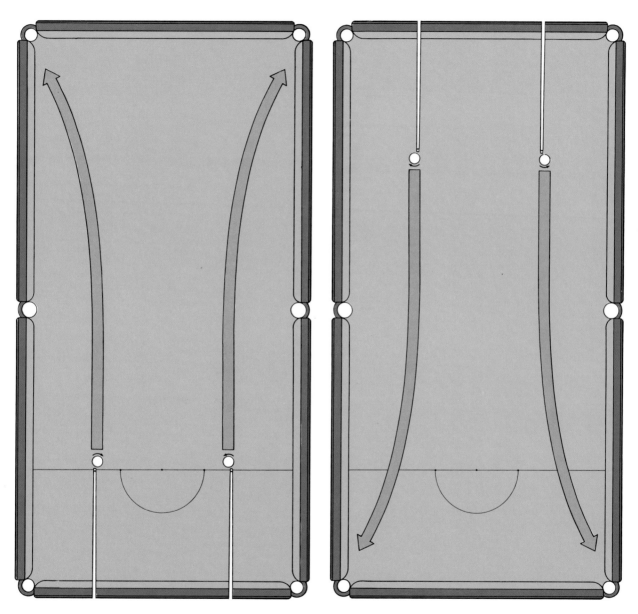

the centre of the table. This is particularly noticeable when you play at an angle against the nap (Fig. 97). Playing the cue ball with side up the table with the nap (Fig. 98), the effect is to take the ball in the direction you would expect.

But when playing against the nap, the ball will tend to go in the opposite direction to the side you have put on it (Fig. 99). It is most important that you master the effects of the nap.

81

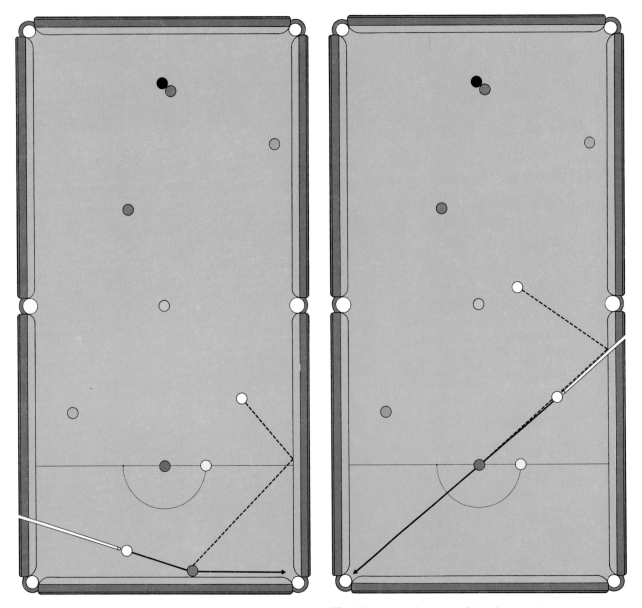

Fig. 100 *Potting red 2. Brown is the next shot.*

Fig. 101 *Potting brown. Red 3 is the next shot.*

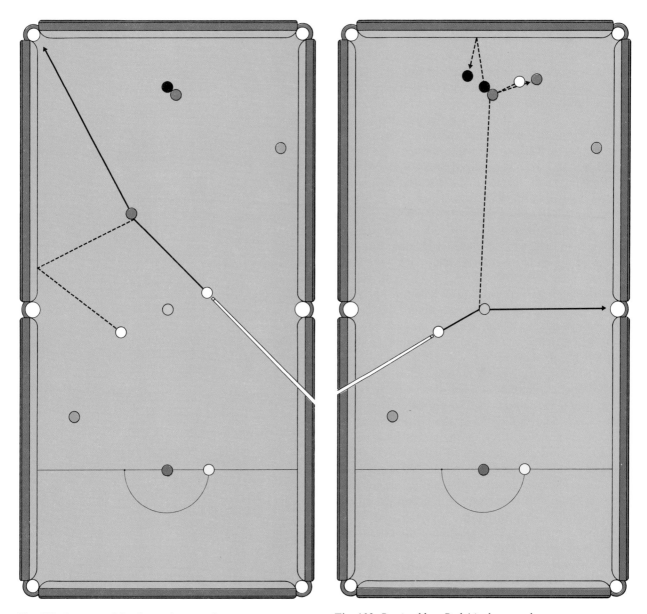

Fig. 102 *Potting red 3. Blue is the next shot.*

Fig. 103 *Potting blue. Red 4 is the next shot.*

towards the top right-hand pocket. The momentum of the white would have been stopped by the black. This obviously required exceptional accuracy. Whereas many people would be concerned just to split the black and red balls, professionals would strive to ensure both finished up in good positions.

I played the shot almost to perfection, but hit the red thinner than planned and almost simultaneously with the black. This left the white and red a lot closer together than I would have liked.

Looking much further ahead, I wanted to play as perfect a position off the yellow as possible to get on the green. Ideally from the red I wanted to get down for one of the colours nearer the yellow. But because the white and red were so close and I could only tap in the red, I had to settle for the black. The next problem I had to face was getting down to the yellow from the black, which was quite a distance – and the further the white has to travel, the greater the margin for error. I delicately soft-screwed the half-ball red into the top right-hand pocket and left myself a thick half-ball pot on the black.

The ideal potting angle for the yellow to get on the green would have been a half-ball, with the white much nearer the brown than I eventually put it. This would leave a natural pot, with the white running off the side cushion and back on the green. As it was, I potted the black into the top left-hand pocket, using top and a little left-hand side to bring the white back into the middle of the table after hitting the top and side cushions. But I finished up in a bad position – just off straight with the yellow.

I had two choices. One was to pot the yellow and screw back up the table in the direction of the blue to try a long-pot green into the bottom left-hand pocket. Or I could go for a strong run-through off the yellow which would take the white off the side and bottom cushions towards the green. Both shots had their advantages and disadvantages.

With the first shot I needed to screw back past the blue to have a reasonable chance of potting the green.

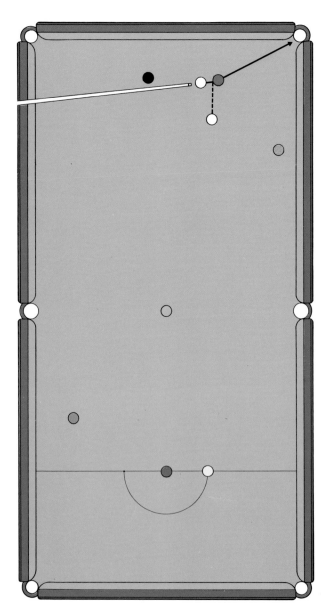

Fig. 104 *Potting red 4. Black is the next shot.*

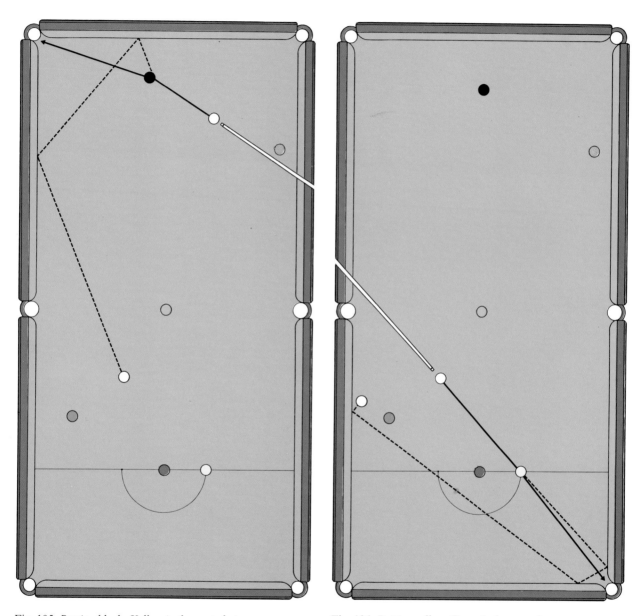

Fig. 105 *Potting black. Yellow is the next shot.*

Fig. 106 *Potting yellow. Green is the next shot.*

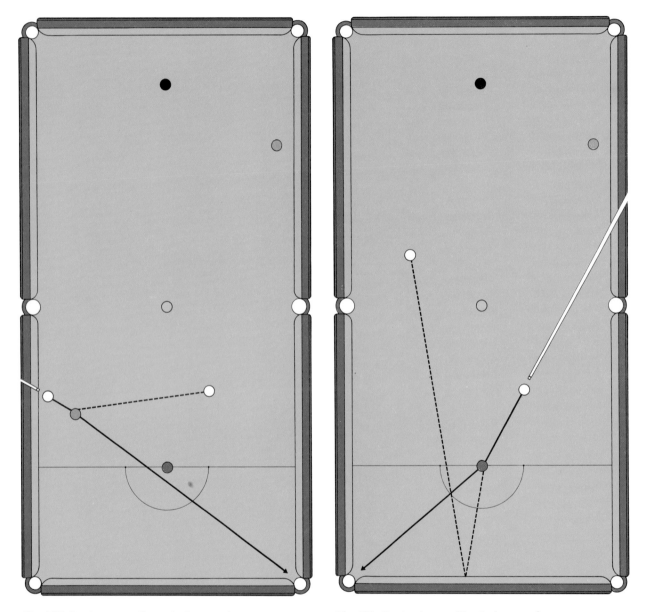

Fig. 107 *Potting green. Brown is the next shot.*

Fig. 108 *Potting brown. Blue is the next shot.*

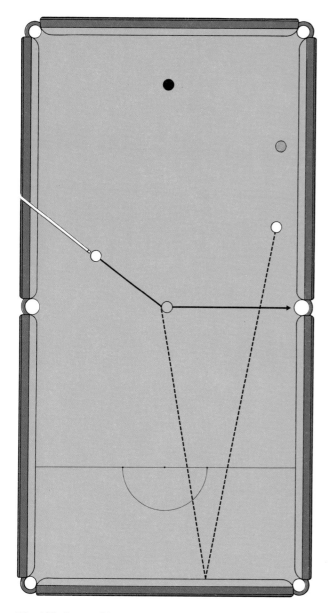

Fig. 109 *Potting blue. Pink is the next shot.*

If I ended up short of the blue, I would have had a very awkward angle on the green – less than a half-ball. As it was, I wanted nothing less than a three-quarter-ball for this long pot. I also had to screw back far enough so I wouldn't have to play the shot with a rest, which meant the white would probably have to come back as far as in line with the pink spot. But a power screw shot of the force I needed could not be judged to perfection – and I had to overplay rather than underplay it. There was another basic objection: as a rule, the longer the pot, the harder the shot. The advantage of this shot was that no matter where I ended up I had a chance of potting the green.

The main advantage of the second shot was that the white would end up a lot closer to the green, although there was a danger I could be too close. Also, as long as I didn't leave the white too short, I had four pockets that I could have had a realistic chance of potting the green into – the top, middle and bottom right-hand and the bottom left-hand. My one worry was that the white might finish up too close to the green.

Now I had to decide. Should I go for the easier shot of screwing down the table and have a more difficult second shot or should I play the difficult positional shot first, knowing that if I played it right, I would be close enough to the green to control the white and play position on the brown, the next ball? I decided to go for the second shot.

I potted a thickish three-quarter-ball yellow with a small amount of right-hand side into the bottom right-hand pocket and with a strong run-through sent the white off two cushions towards the green. At one stage it looked as though the white might cannon on to the green and push it towards the side cushion, which would have been fatal. But it just missed the green on the left side to leave me a perfect, if slightly surprising, position on the green into the same pocket as the yellow. I had visualised having to pot the green into the middle or top right-hand pocket, as it had seemed more likely the white would end up

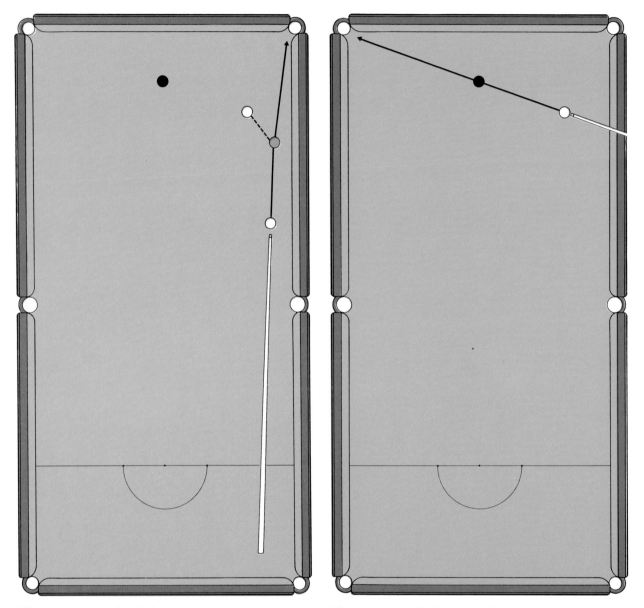

Fig. 110 *Potting pink. Black is the next shot.*

Fig. 111 *Potting black. That's a break of 51.*

in that area near the side cushion – just below the green.

As it was, I had a thickish three-quarter-ball pot on the green, which meant I could run through naturally, sending the white across the table for position on the brown into the opposite bottom corner pocket.

The only slightly difficult ball left was the pink and all I concentrated on here with the brown was to play for a fair position on the blue to enable me to get on the pink afterwards. This meant potting the brown with a good run-through off the bottom cushion to send the white towards the blue.

Having potted the three-quarter-ball brown, I should ideally have ended up just short of the blue. But I overran the shot by a foot or so, which meant I had a slightly tougher positional shot – stunning the white and sending it off the bottom cushion and back towards the pink. As long as I didn't then overrun the white, I was always going to have a chance of the pink into the top right-hand pocket.

The half-ball blue went in, but I could have left the white a lot further from the pink than I did. It meant playing with the rest, although this dis-advantage was cancelled out by the fact that the white and pink were quite close. With a thickish three-quarter-ball pot into the top right-hand pocket, I had a natural run-through off the pink on to the black. This pot into the top left-hand pocket was just off straight and I completed a break of 51.

Summary

This break was completely different from the first, since there were crisis points that required very accurate positional play – not pin-point position, but accurate direction. And I had to get good angles on certain balls to be able to clear the table. If I set up this sequence again, my chances of clearing the table, compared with the first break, would be a lot less.

During this break there were many occasions when it could very easily have come to an end. This is where luck does to an extent play a part in break-building. Also this shows that to make a maximum break of 147 requires enormous accuracy and luck as to how the balls are situated and then split up during the break.

Why not set up these breaks for yourself and see how far you get? You don't have to follow the way I played them exactly. Try to work out different ways of play-ing them. The important point is that you have got to be adaptable and prepared to change course if a particular shot doesn't go as planned.

Chapter 5 Tactical play

Matchplay

If you take snooker seriously, practice isn't just about playing well; it's also a means to an end – competing in and winning matches. Most people are competitive by nature and like to be successful – and so the more you improve your standards, the better you should be in matches. Always play to win, but practise to improve.

There are plenty of players who are fine in practice but who go to pieces when put in a match. I personally revel in matchplay, but that's also partly because I've got a good temperament and enjoy playing in front of an audience. Of course there are pressures on you in a match which wouldn't normally be there – having people watch you, for example, and the pressures and disappointment of losing.

One of the main things to remember is not to get upset or annoyed – easier said than done, I agree! There will be times in a match when your opponent gets lucky or you start to play badly. On the whole, if the general standard of your game is good, luck will often level itself out over a number of frames.

If you get upset, it will not only spoil your own game but will also give your opponent more confidence. And with greater confidence often goes a greater share of the luck, so the situation gets worse instead of better. All in all, it will lead to bad lapses of concentration and, to me, this is unforgivable.

Always keep your feelings inside you if you can – and under control. Sometimes you will feel frustrated, but the great thing is not to show it. Nerves are another problem and there is no magic cure for these. The best way is to force yourself to play as many matches as you can to try to accustom yourself to big games. Everyone, I am sure, must have gone through this stage at some time or another. Even now, I get butterflies in the stomach before the start of a big match, but they go as soon as I get to the table.

Relaxation helps control nerves and it's sound advice to do whatever you find helps you relax before or in between matches – and here I certainly don't include drugs or drink! These will only impair your vision and your ability to think clearly, both of which are vital for your game. It has become a standing joke that my hotel bedroom is lined with 'Space Invader' machines, but I do enjoy playing them and they help me to relax and also concentrate.

At certain points in a match, the pressure tends to build up as you reach a crucial stage. Certain balls become big pressure shots, which you are always more liable to miss. It then boils down to who is the most consistent under pressure.

It's not a question of how good your best is, but how good your worst is. One bad spell in a match can finish you. So it is much better to be consistently good than to be erratic – with flashes of brilliance. You might well have a purple patch, but that isn't guaranteed to win you the match as much as a bad patch is to lose it.

When you start to lose frames and the going gets really tough, that's when your ability to fight comes in. I never think I'm out of a game until the ball goes down that makes it physically impossible for me to win.

When the chips are down, there is a great tendency to take risks and try to get back into the game. Don't be tempted. It is far better to wait and hope your opponent gets over-confident. When things are going well, a player will feel on top of the world and may attempt too many ambitious shots – and that's where your chance comes to get back into the game. You must try to take whatever chances you are given; there may not be too many. In world class snooker, sometimes you only get one chance per frame.

Obviously you must try not to give your opponent too many chances, either. If things aren't going too well, it's often better to play a safety shot than to attempt any ambitious one to get out of trouble and find you've let your opponent back in.

Having said that you shouldn't take risks, you certainly don't want to adopt a totally defensive attitude, either. That will never win you matches. You will have to judge the situation as you find it and weigh up the percentages on each shot before you decide. Particularly when the competition standard is not that high, a good break will win you the frame and you must be prepared to go for it.

The hallmark of a good player is being able to think under pressure and not panic. When you are faced with a difficult shot and can't make up your mind whether to go for it or not, what should you do? The obvious first thought is whether you would have played the shot in practice, although in that situation you would not be under any pressure.

I suggest you ask yourself the following questions: Can I pot this ball? What are the chances of getting it? Will I be guaranteed a continuation of the break afterwards? Is it worth the risk for the opening I might give my opponent if I miss? If you can answer in the affirmative to these questions, then by all means go for it.

You often find the same shots cropping up at different times in the game, but depending on the circumstances you will have to decide whether to play a particular shot or not, even though you have done it successfully earlier in the game. Your decision will depend on where the remaining balls are positioned, how many points are left on the table, how many you need to win, how many your opponent needs to win and so on.

This part of the game is all down to tactics – and it's your choice that counts. You must weigh up in your mind whether you are prepared to take a calculated risk or not. That's what makes a good tactician. You can never advise someone on what shot to play. In the end, it's down to the player.

That's what for me makes matchplay so exciting. If you make the right decision, everyone applauds. Equally, everyone will be quick to criticise the wrong decision. As far as I'm concerned, it's an exciting prospect; it's just down to you.

In all this there is, I'm afraid, another imponderable – the frame of mind you are in at the time. You may be faced with a shot that you should get, but something inside tells you that you just don't fancy it and you won't get it – and sure enough you don't. Sometimes this happens when you're already down on the shot and cueing up. If this is the case, get up and start again.

Everyone has favourite shots. If you look at a shot and feel you can get it, by following your instinct you will often make it, even though it may be a poor percentage shot. You have to rely on your own judgement.

A few final words on matchplay. If you are serious about your game, enter as many competitions as you can, whether at club or regional level. You don't have to be left out because you are a junior or because you feel your standard isn't good enough yet. If you are under 19, for example, you can go in for the British Junior Championships. There is an Under-16 Boys Championships as well.

You must always make a point of playing people you don't know – and therefore not knowing how they play. This is the best test of how much your game is improving and will help you develop a better temperament for tournaments. Never be scared of an opponent. It's up to you what you do and how you play; it should never be up to your opponent. When you get on to the table, there's only one person in the game at that stage.

In some ways matches will improve your game better than practice. I obviously learnt a vast amount in my formative years of playing snooker, but I have now reached the point where I don't learn so much from practice. What I do learn, I learn from playing matches – and it's mainly tactical. Of course I still make sure the standard of my technique is maintained. If necessary I will spend time correcting a fault that might develop over a long period.

I believe the value of matches is that your mistakes are punished and that alone brings it home to you more. For the same reason you tend to learn more when you lose than when you win. When you win, you

91

often overlook where you went wrong or the bad shots you played. When you lose, you are forced to analyse where you went wrong – or you would simply go on losing.

Safety play

Safety play is an important part of matchplay. But you shouldn't spend too much time practising it out of context or you will be in danger of hindering your natural game. There is obviously little point in perfecting safety techniques if you still can't pot balls consistently. You can only win matches by scoring points.

There are basically three types of safety play tactics. There are those shots that will put your opponent in an awkward position and maybe force him to give you an opening with the next shot. This can be labelled attacking safety play. Equally you may have to play shots to try to stop your opponent from getting an opening. These are not as good as attacking tactics since your opponent still has the initiative. This type of play involves defensive, stalling tactics.

The third type of safety play can incorporate both the other two. It is used when the frame is already well beyond your reach. Perhaps you are also several frames down and your opponent is playing well. Then you can deliberately try to upset his potting rhythm by denying him potting opportunities. This will, of course, upset your own potting rhythm as well. If however, you are not putting your game together that well anyway, the effect on you will be less serious. This tactic doesn't always work, but when you're losing you've got to try all possibilities.

Safety play involves a high degree of ball control. It is similar to positional play except you are not so concerned about the position of the object ball. The weight of the shot you play also becomes extremely important.

The first shot of the game is a safety shot and can be played in different ways, highlighting the difference between defensive and attacking safety play (Figs. 112

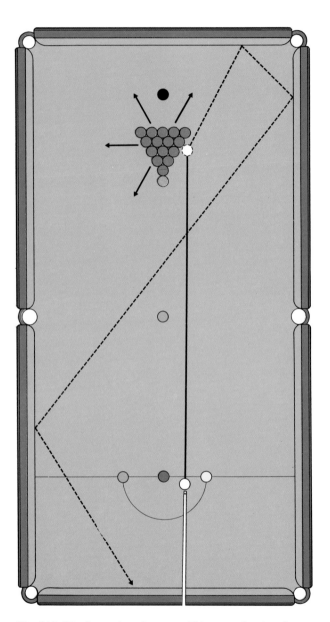

Fig. 112 *The first safety shot you will have to play in a frame is on the opening break. The one shown here is a positive safety shot.*

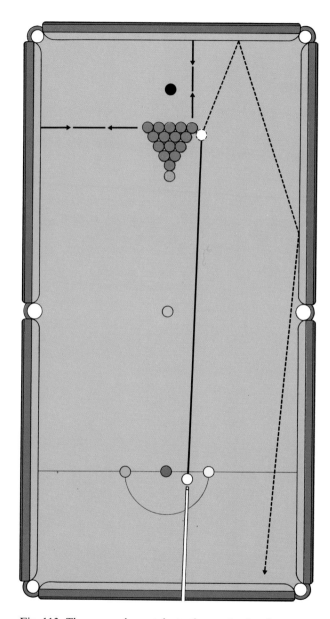

Fig. 113 *The approach you take to the opening break can vary. As is demonstrated by this shot, you can adopt a negative attitude.*

and 113). If from the baulk you clip the pack of reds gently with the white without disturbing them much, the white will come back down the table. But you are not gaining any advantage from the shot since your opponent can do exactly the same thing if he wants to. This is definitely a defensive safety shot.

The better shot to play here is to aim to hit the pack thicker to spread them. This may mean taking a risk; but if the white ends up where intended (on the baulk cushion behind the green), you will have left your opponent in a very difficult situation.

One elementary safety rule is to keep the white as far away as you can from the object ball, since distance always opens up more chances for error. In many cases, too, you will make your opponent's shot a lot harder if the cue ball ends up on the cushion.

At the start of most games, there is a general pattern of safety play. Both players are trying to gain the advantage by keeping the white down in baulk and attempting to put the opponent in an awkward position where he cannot do the same. This is done by clipping the pack of reds and disturbing just one or two at a time. Usually one side of the table becomes quite difficult to negotiate, whereas the other is often free of reds.

When doing this, try to put your opponent in positions where the side of the pack from which it is easier to get back down the table is covered up by the baulk colours. Your opponent then has to play into a potentially more dangerous area.

Apart from these few principles, the best sort of safety shot is a snooker.

The snooker

There are many ways of setting up a snooker and it would be impossible for me to give you examples of each. So much depends on the general state of the game and the position of all the balls left on the table. I can, however, provide you with some useful guidelines.

When trying to get a snooker, for instance with

just the pink and black left on the table, it is far better to have the white just behind the black and the pink somewhere down the table than the other way round. There is a much better chance of getting out of this snooker if the balls are the other way round.

Try also to make sure your opponent has to play off at least two cushions – the more cushions the better – since there is then more chance for error.

If the pack of reds is still pretty well intact, there is little advantage of playing a snooker, since your opponent has a relatively easy task to hit somewhere on the pack. If you can, however, snooker him on the reds when they are scattered. This is an excellent shot since it will open the table up for your next shot, whether he gets out of the snooker successfully or not.

Shots to nothing

These shots are particularly advantageous because they give you two chances. You can play them when there is a difficult pot on and the cue ball is going to come back naturally into a safe position if you miss thereby denying your opponent a chance of the pot.

In conclusion

By now you should have a broader understanding of this fascinating game – you may even have become an addict like me. But don't let your enthusiasm for success make you too hasty; you need a sound foundation on which to build success, so spend time perfecting your technique, prepare yourself psychologically for the contest and then approach the table ready to win.

Index